The Brightness around Him

THE BRIGHTNESS AROUND HIM

A Spiritual Odyssey

∼

JIM STRAHAN
with Mike Meeker

RESOURCE *Publications* • Eugene, Oregon

THE BRIGHTNESS AROUND HIM
A Spiritual Odyssey

Copyright © 2015 Jim Strahan. All rights reserved. Except for brief quotations in critical publications or reviews, no part of this book may be reproduced in any manner without prior written permission from the publisher. Write: Permissions, Wipf and Stock Publishers, 199 W. 8th Ave., Suite 3, Eugene, OR 97401.

Resource Publications
An Imprint of Wipf and Stock Publishers
199 W. 8th Ave., Suite 3
Eugene, OR 97401

www.wipfandstock.com

ISBN 13: 978-1-4982-2981-4

Manufactured in the U.S.A.   09/16/2015

Visit isgodfair.com and passitforward.life

Unless otherwise indicated, scripture taken from the New King James Version®. Copyright © 1982 by Thomas Nelson. Used by permission. All rights reserved.

Scripture quotations labeled NIV are from the Holy Bible, New International Version Copyright © 1973, 1978 by Biblica, Inc. Used by permission of Zondervan. All rights reserved worldwide. http://www.zondervan.com

Scripture quotations labeled ESV are from The Holy Bible, English Standard (Version 8 ESVK), copyright © 2001 by Crossway, a publishing ministry of Good News Publishers. Used by permission. All rights reserved. ESV Text Edition: 2007

Scripture quotations labeled KJV are from The Holy Bible, King James Version

The internet addresses, email addresses, and phone numbers in this book are accurate at the time of publication. They are provided as a resource. Resource Publications does not endorse them or vouch for their content or permanence.

Contents

Foreword | vii

Introduction: I Remember Now | ix

1. Eyes of a Child | 1
2. So Flows the Current | 8
3. Behind the Waterfall | 20
4. Gradual Understanding | 28
5. Counting Clouds | 45
6. Breakthrough | 53
7. Holding Faith | 64
8. Where We Once Stood | 70
9. Beyond This Moment | 76
10. Bloom | 104
11. May You Run | 115

Epilogue | 125
Appendix: Notes from Let's Talk Bible | 129

Foreword

Although I am an ordinary man, I've had some extraordinary experiences, and my hope is that writing them down and evaluating them will be beneficial to more people than just me. A few of my experiences are unusual enough to border on the unbelievable, and after struggling for five decades and coming to the realization that our personal stories can be a big help to others, I consider the risk of being misunderstood or marginalized by some a good trade-off for any new-found peace provided to others.

I am especially grateful to family and friends who have believed in me and given so much encouragement. To others who are not so sure, I completely understand—because I myself struggled with these experiences and their implications. I've kept most of them to myself over the years out of fear they would make others feel uncomfortable around me. However, as I approach the backside of my life's journey, I cannot keep this treasure buried any longer.

Introduction

I Remember Now

~

Research indicates that talking about self triggers the same pleasure centers in the brain as does love, money and food. In this brief introduction I'll test that theory, and at the end of it, I'll let you know if I've been able to derive the full intrinsic value that self-disclosure might produce. I will start with a casual discussion of a few common life experiences. Without knowing the rest of my story in the pages that follow, a case could be made that my life has been consumed with the big three listed above, and there is not much more to tell other than how the ranking of their importance has reversed with age. (Older guys will see the humor.)

Seriously, I wish I could tell you about some great accomplishments which would distinguish me from others, but unfortunately, none will be found in my life. However, in the chapters that follow, I will brag about the One who is responsible for an incredible inner strength developed in me over a lifetime of training – an eternal strength that no man can touch or reproduce. Before the book is over, I'll also show how that strength can be yours if you have not already received it. But before we move into that arena, let's start with a cursory summary of my life as an outsider might view it without the knowledge of the transformation going on inside of me.

I was raised in a blue-collar neighborhood in San Antonio, Texas. My father was a police officer, and my mother stayed at home raising me and my three sisters. We didn't have a lot of money, but our needs were met and love was plentiful.

Back then (the late 50s and early 60s) there were nine other boys in the neighborhood about my age, and my childhood was filled with terrific friends and characters. At one point, the group almost made up an entire

I Remember Now

Pop Warner football team—we even won our conference and played in the city championship. We were very active kids and loved the outdoors. There was a creek and a swamp within a mile or two of our homes, and if we weren't playing football, we were either fishing, camping, exploring, or, well, sleeping.

As all good outdoorsmen, we ate what we caught or killed, except for that armadillo. Seven of us had gone camping in the Stonewall area in central Texas. We planned to kill a deer the first evening for dinner but didn't have any luck. We went to bed hungry and rose early the next morning determined to fulfill our destiny and fill our stomachs. However, several little boys stalking deer through the rock, cedar and live oaks didn't yield any edible results. The only animals we stirred up were some armadillos. Later in the morning one of the guys remembered eating armadillo at a county fair, and we were so hungry. However, after we shot one, a few unborn babies appeared during the cleaning process, and that sadness robbed us of our manhood and our appetites.

We left without eating and headed back to my friend's grandparent's home. They lived in a farm house about two and a half miles from where we had camped. We soon forgot about our lack of success and gorged on homemade bread, butter and all kinds of jellies and jams from the last harvest. We recovered our manhood the next day after camping on the banks of the Pedernales River that evening. We were determined to catch and eat our own food, and by god, that's what we did, well, sort of.

We took some poles and nets to fish and sane the river and mud holes along the banks, but as it turned out, we didn't need to do all of that work. During the evening we spied a farmer on the other side of the river setting his throw and trout lines. After a brief early morning swim the next day, we enjoyed some of the best fish we never caught. Looking back, I guess we were mischievous at times, but overall, we never hurt anyone, and I couldn't think of a better group of friends to grow up with.

Of course, there were girls in the neighborhood too, whose physical differences were the subject of many conversations, and some embarrassing moments. My best friend found some magazines and stored them in an old tire on the side of his house. One morning his father caught us reading them, well, not really reading them. At that moment we just knew our lives were over, because in our neighborhood parents had no problem using the rod to correct and all of us feared the wrath of our fathers the most. But instead of coming down hard on us, his dad took the material and then let us off the hook, but not without a painful lecture about manhood. Real men were not supposed to sneak around and that was a sure indicator that this type of behavior was wrong.

I would describe my teenage years as fairly normal too. Since I had so much practice in backyard sports, I played football, basketball and ran track in junior high and high school. There's not much to write about here, except that basketball paid for some of my college education. Also, despite my creativity in high-jumping over the bar backward at my first track meet in the fifth grade, a few years later, a fellow by the name of Fosberry won the high jump at the Olympics and the Fosberry Flop became the name of the new style instead of the Strahan Cannonball as my competition called it. Now, would you rather be a cannonball, or a flop? I don't know why cannonball didn't stick; the only difference between him and me was a mere foot. Yeesh, life is so unfair at times. I could have been famous.

I quit football after my freshman year in high school. I loved the game so much, but didn't care for the head coach. With the encouragement of the basketball coach, I concentrated on two sports instead of three. He told me I could play and possibly start my sophomore year on a basketball team that had won the State championship a few years prior. We both knew I had no chance at the starting quarterback position on the football team until my senior year, because there was an All-American one year ahead of those of us competing for the position.

That football coach and I didn't speak much after I quit. However, about thirty years later and a few days before he died, from his hospital bed he told my cousin that I would have been another Tommy Kramer had I stayed with it. Tommy became the starter at our high school after our senior class graduated and was voted the State's MVP. Later, he became an all-American at Rice and an all-pro with the Minnesota Vikings. I was surprised by the coach's comments, that he even remembered me, and I often wonder how all of that would have worked out had I stayed. I don't pretend to think I would have ever been as good as Tommy. And I do not bring this up as something to brag about either, but rather as an introduction to another story I'm not so proud of. But first, let's finish my schooling.

After my first year of college basketball, I realized that playing at a professional level was not in the cards for me. Even though I knew I could have been on an athletic scholarship for the next three years, I elected to leave sports altogether and make some money working while I pursued my education. I had an academic scholarship too at the time and was able to have a savings account for the first time in my life. After seeing the advantages of having a little pocket change, I decided I needed more. It was a great move, as I found a part time job at UPS in their engineering department. By the time I graduated, I had a girlfriend, a car, two motorcycles, a good paying job, and no debt.

That girlfriend turned into a wife, and that part-time job turned into a career. My wife and I eventually had two children and she did a great job of raising them while I spent much of my time at work. My career took us from San Antonio to Dallas, to Salt Lake City, and on to Nashville before returning back to Texas. We now live in Boerne.

Our two children have been a great joy for us and we could not have asked for more. My daughter married a civil engineer, who is a former US Army Ranger. They live just north of Dallas and recently blessed us with our first grandson. I could not ask for a better son-in-law, and we are very proud of our daughter as she recently finished her doctorate in physical therapy. My son just married a very beautiful woman and they are now living in South Carolina working as research chemists. Both have their PhD's and we are proud of them as well.

I've had a good life, made lots of great friends, and consider myself to be extremely blessed. I still love to camp, fish and explore . . . that's not changed. What has changed is that I won't stalk deer out of season, fish illegally, (did I mention that?) or steal another man's catch. I do cheat at golf by fluffing up my ball or taking an occasional mulligan, but only when I really need it. So there it is—a kid who loved sports, went to school, got a job, married, had some kids, worked hard, still says bad words on the golf course, and is now ready to retire. I definitely need more time on the course so that I can straighten up my swing. I figure that having a better game should make me a better person too, because then, I won't lose my cool as often and give in to my natural inclination to apply accurate but inappropriate descriptors to errant strikes. Words like, "that was a poor shot" don't always express my true inner feelings.

I'm a plain and ordinary guy, blessed with friends and loved by family. Just like millions of other men, we aren't famous cannonballs, but we certainly aren't flops. And when we can summarize our life's accomplishments in a couple of pages or less, we don't tend to think of ourselves as all that special. However, despite the outward appearances, the occasional errant shot or outbursts of frustration on the course of life, I have discovered something extraordinary working inside of me, and I have good reasons to suspect that it is working inside of you too. Furthermore, I am convinced that one day it will transform us into something so wonderful and special that it will exceed everyone's expectations, even those we've disappointed in this life, like my football coach, that fisherman/farmer, and maybe even you after slogging through the first few pages of this book.

I'll close this section with some words of wisdom hot off the press: Love, money and food are much better stimulators than talking about self . . . I think I'll go have some pizza. And now we will end the small talk and outward appearances and reveal in the opening chapter what has been working inside of me . . . and you.

1

Eyes of a Child

~

When I was seven years old I had an amazing experience that would forever change me and send me on a remarkable journey. It happened on an ordinary night after my family had retired to bed. My sister and I went to sleep on a pad made on the floor in front of the family's small black and white television set. I don't recall what we watched before we fell asleep; it could have been *Rawhide* with trail boss Gil Favors and his assistant Rowdy Yates, or *Bonanza* with Adam, Little Joe and Hoss Cartwright. I probably fell asleep sometime between eight-thirty and nine as was our routine on school nights. Some hours later, the safe and familiar were interrupted by the extraordinary.

It was the sound of creaking wood right next to me that woke me up. I heard footsteps on our hardwood floor and was paralyzed with fear. In those days people did not lock their doors at night, and because most did not have air conditioning, the only thing separating us from the outside was screened windows. My first thought was that some unwelcomed person had entered our house and was now standing over me and my sister.

I was petrified! I knew it wasn't a bad dream or nightmare; this was the real thing. The adrenaline was pumping and I was as awake and alert as I am now. Thinking it might be a burglar, I lay motionless hoping he would take whatever he wanted and leave. If I yelled out for help, I thought it might put me in greater danger since the intruder was so close and my dad was asleep down the hall. I remember thinking this man could really hurt me and my sister before my dad could get there, so I decided to remain still and silent. These thoughts were racing through my head, when suddenly,

I felt the strange sensation of my body coming off the floor and moving in an upward direction.

I thought this sinister person had taken my life, and I was heading for heaven. As a Baptist, I knew that heaven was up, and the bad place was down. I also remembered having asked God into my heart at the age of four, so I was confident I was going to the good place. Looking back, I'm amazed at the volume of thoughts and feelings that passed through my mind and body so quickly. I guess it was the adrenaline. I went from sheer terror to pure happiness in a matter of seconds with the thought of going to heaven. I immediately started wondering what it would look like and all I could think of was pearly gates. I thought about opening my eyes and watching my flight from earth, but the thought of that kind of height scared me, so I kept my eyes closed until the trip was over.

The sensation of going upward lasted only a few seconds until I felt myself stop. I had arrived! I could feel myself smile wondering who would welcome me. Maybe I was going to see a real angel! Then, with my eyes still closed, and not really knowing what would happen, I heard a voice speak these words: "It is I, when I died on the cross for you."

The fear was gone, and I opened my eyes. It was Jesus who had entered that room. He had picked me up off the floor and put me on a bed next to where I had been sleeping. He walked across the room and turned around and showed me the nail scars in his hands and feet, then turned, and showed me the scar in his side. He was wearing a white robe and literally lit up the room so that I could see him and everything in it very plainly. I could see that my sister was still asleep on the floor.

Several people who know my story have asked what he looked like. His brown hair was slightly long and wavy, and his beard appeared to be thin, although I wasn't really concentrating on that part of him; I kept looking into his eyes. He had a long thin nose and face with sunken brown eyes and heavy eyelashes. Except for the brightness around him, he looked rather normal. To be honest, when I saw the image on the Shroud of Turin for the first time, I told myself that was him. But I know the shroud's authenticity can't be 100 percent verified, so all I'm saying is that if I had any ability to draw something other than a straight line with the help of a ruler, my sketch of him would look exactly like that image. I have also described him as looking like an older George Harrison with less hair and a longer, thinner nose.

Eyes of a Child

After exposing his side, he was gone, and I was back down on the floor. It is hard to describe how I felt when it was over. It was like falling in love for the first time, but much stronger. As I laid there on the floor, all I could do was tell him how much I loved him and appreciated his coming to me. His love had instantly crushed my heart. Tears still flow whenever I think about it, even after all these years—they spring from the overwhelming realization of the undeserved and inescapable love I felt from him.

The next morning I told my parents what happened, and they immediately called over our minister. We kept quiet about my experience except for close Christian friends for obvious reasons; who would believe such a story from a child? And I have remained somewhat quiet about it during my life, only telling my closest Christian friends. I made one exception: relating it to my church once in Salt Lake City. I had been asked to lead the Communion portion of the service, and I thought the timing was right to tell everyone about the vision. When it was over, I knew it hadn't been such a good idea after all. I remember tearing up and having great difficulty staying composed as I relayed my experience. After the service was over, only one person came up to me to speak about it, and I took that to mean most were uncomfortable with it. I knew my family and friends were embarrassed, and I really didn't want to put them through that. I was disappointed and silently asked the Lord where I had gone wrong.

Finally, one stranger introduced himself and told me that his son had a similar experience, and they were anticipating his calling into the ministry. I felt a little better. I know of only one other person with a similar story and I met him years later at a church we attended in Franklin, Tennessee. He and his wife were both medical doctors, and he told me that he had seen Jesus twice, but who would believe us?

For the next thirty-three years I continued to thank the Lord for what he had done, but I also had some questions. Why me? And what was I supposed to *do*? I didn't feel a call to be a minister, had no desire to be one not having been blessed with the skills required for the job. The only thing I was good at was math, jumping over a bar backwards and throwing a leather object through a hoop – truly important stuff. I realized how sad that was, but I was always hopeful I would eventually find some greater purpose to my life, as soon as he told why I had been selected. As life rolled along, and it became increasingly apparent I was no saint, and that I was not heading for anything other than an ordinary life, the questions began to pile up. The vision just didn't make any sense.

My frustration back then is hard to explain. I mean, I met Jesus! Most people would give anything to meet him, and that should have been enough to spur me on to some great calling, knowing that he really was who he said he was. Looking back, I was too young and too dumb to understand my advantage. I completely understand why it is difficult for people to believe in a loving Creator given the harsh realities of this world. How can we know with certainty that God isn't just some hopeful figment of our imagination? And if he does exist, what is he like? Does he even care? At the tender age of seven, I was handed the answers to some of the most difficult questions ever asked by mankind. However, I needed more time to appreciate the human condition, his love for us, and the miracle of faith. At age fourteen, I received my first reality check, and it marked another turning point in my life.

For the first seven years after the Lord's appearance, my heart burned with love for him, and my confidence soared as I knew he was with me at all times. However, my confidence was rocked at age fourteen when prayers for my mother's health and our family's financial condition weren't answered as I had expected. During that time I watched my mom cry in pain daily, for months! I watched as one of her legs shriveled and became noticeably shorter than the other. We didn't know what was wrong, or where to go for help.

Additionally, we were poor and doctor visits were limited. My dad had two jobs most of the time, and sometimes three, just to put food on the table. It hurt me to watch my mother and father struggle. To make matters worse, I was going to school with some friends whose parents were some of the wealthiest in the city. It didn't seem fair that good people like my parents were having so many trials while others less saintly seemed to be enjoying the pleasures of life. What had my parents done wrong? I remember asking for the Lord's help, but relief didn't come, and I became very angry with him.

In frustration, one day I took my Bible outside and got ready to throw it as far as I could. I told him exactly what I thought about him and his weak-kneed followers, most of whom I thought would believe anything no matter if it were true or not! Certainly prayer didn't work because he didn't answer them! I was hurt because he didn't seem to care. With Bible in hand, I cocked my arm in anger ready it throw it over the fence into the back alley with the rest of the trash. But at the last second, I stopped; I couldn't do it.

I went back inside and my parents called our minister because they knew how upset I had become.

Our pastor was kind enough to come to the house and pray with me, but given my anger, it was absolutely no help. There was no one who could console me, and I felt like a big fool for believing in God. I cried some bitter tears.

Eventually, I calmed down emotionally and began to analyze my situation. I had not been able to toss the Bible because I could not deny the fact that he died on the cross for me. I also recalled the love I had felt in his presence and the overwhelming peace, like everything was going to be okay. It was totally opposite of the emotions I was feeling at the time. I didn't realize it, but can now see with great clarity that I had come to a crossroad in my life.

There were three paths I could have taken, but two of them, the ones that seemed more sensible at the time—the ones I *wanted* to take—were blocked. First, Jesus had removed the path of atheism, as I couldn't possibly deny his existence. Secondly, he also removed the path of the agnostic by showing me how he had laid down his life for others, the greatest gift anyone could give to another. There was no way around the two truths that God was real, and he was good. With those words ringing in my head, "It is I when I died on the cross for you" he removed all other choices and pointed me toward a path where I would eventually find hope, peace and comfort. I wasn't smart enough to figure it out on my own. I needed help, and I received it.

I had a free will, but it was no match against the power of his love. This was not the path I would have chosen, and he knew it. And only because of his intervention was I spared a dead end journey to fantasy, friction and frustration. It was like a blindfolded child swinging the stick and missing the piñata over and over again until receiving guidance from the parent.

I began to weep again, but this time because I was so sorry for the things I had said about him. In humility, I apologized, confessing my limited knowledge and lack of understanding. At that moment, I decided to trust him. Anyone who could do what he did for me is worth believing. I was now prepared to walk down the path of faith keeping three navigation points always in view: There is a Creator. He is good. He knows more than I do.

With my weak knees strengthened, I began my journey again, this time with much more confidence. Of course, I still had much to learn and seven years later my faith would be tried again. This first test came in circumstances beyond my control, the health and finances of the ones I loved. The next test involved my own decisions. (And by the way, my mother eventually had surgery and the pinched nerve was found and fixed. Also, all bills were paid, and we never missed a meal. Our prayers really were answered, just not as quickly or as dramatically as I had desired.)

In my late teenage years and into my early twenties, I felt almost invincible. I knew the Lord was with me and I knew I was destined for something special, because with him, anything was possible. In high school I was a member of the National Honor Society, the Student Council, an officer in the Fellowship of Christian Athletes, and I won athletic and scholastic scholarships. Everything seemed to be going my way.

During this time I met a girl at church and we decided to get married. On the outside, it seemed perfect. She had succeeded me as president of our youth group and we just knew it was right having the support of our families, friends, the church, and God. However, the fairy tale ended rather quickly after a year of struggling with little money and me attempting to finish college while working a full time job.

Failure in marriage was hard to accept. What happened? I thought his hand was upon me. And when it mattered most, prayer didn't seem to work, again! Disappointment and heartache were followed by frustration, and I found myself apologizing once more for becoming so upset about unanswered prayer. But my anger didn't last long this time, since I knew it wasn't his fault. Immaturity and poor choices were the real problems, and unfortunately, it affected our families and friends.

After this humbling experience, I left the church I had attended for many years. I was ready to move on with my life knowing that God was not a genie in a bottle who I could conjure at will. And clearly, I wasn't invincible. I began to realize his promise was not that he would make everything perfect for me in this life, but rather, he would be with me even at my weakest moments and at the worst of times. I learned that the phrase "All things work together for our good" was a terrible paraphrase of scripture. The best modern translation says ". . . in all things, God works for the good of those who love him" (Romans 8:28). Disease, divorce and death are not good things, but even in them, he promises to work for our good.

It took me a long time to gain this perspective. It would not have been possible were it not for him showing up in my bedroom in a visual display of his love. It would not have been possible without him blocking the paths to atheism and agnosticism. He knew I would not have what it would take to live a life of faith, or complete what he had called me to do without intervention on his part. I was too weak and ignorant to figure this out on my own. For those reasons, I knew at that point in my life his vision had accomplished one very important thing: it had solidified my faith. For that, I was extremely grateful. However, I knew there was more, much more, and I decided to relax, enjoy the comforts in what I had learned, and wait for his timing to reveal what I was supposed to do with that great vision.

2

So Flows the Current

~

I am sure most would have handled my experiences much better than I did. I am slow and stubborn at times. Given what I've received, I've always said that if St. Paul were alive today, he would have been a much happier man knowing he wasn't the least among us anymore. Like Paul, I saw Jesus, but I'm no saint. And the conviction gets worse when I think about how he has proved his love for me on so many occasions, and walked with me through this life.

I hope it's clear why I prayed over darn near everything in life. I never thought about any other way of living. I didn't always receive answers I wanted, and in at least one case, I probably blew some golden opportunities—like when I quite football during high school. It was a very dramatic time. I couldn't sleep at night from the pressure of coaches pulling me in two different directions with the head basketball coach suggesting I might be better off concentrating full time on the court and my father and others urging me to stay on the gridiron. The self-generated pressure within me to succeed was intense, and I don't really know how to explain or describe it, except that football was dominating my life and I felt the need to get away from it.

After leaving the program before spring training in my freshman year, I knew I had one small window of opportunity to return to the team before two-a-day practices began in August. The day before the August drills began, I felt like I was going to explode inside. So I did what I always did when faced with what I felt was a big decision in my life—I turned to Jesus and asked for guidance. I found the only place I could go to be alone—in the top of a large tree in our backyard, and I began to pray. I knew he would hear me and I devised a way out of my predicament. I told the Lord how I felt, and asked that if it were better for me to play football, then please send over the head coach and the quarterback coach to my house, so I would know what to do. It was around four in the afternoon and I knew there was not much chance of them coming. I could tell my parents that I had prayed about it, and the Lord, not having answered, would put the issue to bed.

I felt so relieved after I came down out of that tree. I went inside and immediately told my mother what I had prayed. As I left her room and began walking back to mine, the doorbell rang. I was so shocked that I acted a bit rude when I opened the front door to see both football coaches standing there. It was a very awkward moment. I didn't invite them in, nor give them a chance to talk. I just told them I would be at practice the next day. They said "Okay," and left.

When I closed the door, I was both glad and sad that God had answered my audacious prayer. A week later I quit football for good, because nothing had changed. I didn't stick around long enough to reap the rewards. The head coach was enraged and wanted to kick me out of all athletic programs at the school, but the basketball coach seemed to understand and kept me on his hoops squad. Those two had coached together at a previous high school where they had won a football state championship. The basketball coach had been close to a player who died from a head injury and he told me privately that he had lost a great deal of enthusiasm for the game of football because of it. I got the impression he was having difficulties with the football coach as well.

I continued with basketball and track, and high school turned out well for me anyway. In hindsight, it probably—no, it *would have* been better had I stayed with football, given God's answer. But it wasn't the end of the world. Over the next several years I had time to think about that blown opportunity, and the next time I faced an important decision, I listened to God's answer, and followed his advice. The Lord knows our weaknesses and he let me learn from football, a mere game, so that I would make better choices later, when it really did count.

About twenty years later, now married with two little ones, I found myself in another pressure cooker. I was working for UPS as an industrial engineer. The desire to succeed was intense, and until a move to Dallas, my career was moving in the right direction. I left a small district in San Antonio where I had a good reputation and moved to one of the larger districts in the company where the operations were much more difficult, and the engineering talent much more competitive. In Dallas, I had been working long hours but began to think I was not having much of an impact. I began to have second thoughts and felt that maybe I'd do better with a teaching career. There wasn't near as much money, but I needed to feel some success, and it just wasn't happening in Dallas.

As the self-inflicted pressure began to mount inside once again, I was approached by another company, RPS, and they offered me a job. I prayed about jumping ship and told the Lord I was going to do it if he did not intervene. Later, I determined it was okay to leave UPS since I wasn't hearing anything from him.

The day I tried to quit, I felt very sick inside. I had been with the company about fifteen years and this was a major move for me. My boss told me to head over to Human Resources to make my resignation official. When I arrived, the HR Manager met with me and told me take a few days off; he was not accepting my resignation. He told me I was well thought of and could move to any manager job in the district when I returned. I began to feel a little better about myself.

I left the HR office confused about what to do next. I began driving around north Dallas and praying aloud in my car. I told him this was such a big decision and I needed to know if he was speaking and if it would be better for me and my family to stay with the company. Looking back, it was almost exactly like the situation I faced years before, and the prayer for guidance was the same. I must have driven and prayed for about an hour and I had no idea where I was. Finally, I pulled into a 7-Eleven convenience store, needing to calm down and get something to drink.

As I began to get out of my car, another vehicle pulled up beside me and an old friend from UPS in San Antonio jumped out and called me by name. I hadn't seen this older gentleman in the ten years since he'd left UPS to become the head of Customer Service and Sales at Tex Pac, one of the largest delivery companies in Texas at that time. He quickly came over and shook my hand. Then he began telling me how much he regretted leaving UPS. He said the pressure had gotten to him but it would have been better if he had just stayed.

I was so stunned by the direct answer that I didn't say much about the decision I was facing. All I wanted to do was jump back in the car and shout my gratitude for the Lord's care. I didn't hesitate to call the HR Manager back and tell him of my mistake. UPS took me back and about eight months later, I was promoted to an Industrial Engineering Division

So Flows the Current

Manager position over the States of Utah and Idaho. The pressure on the job never let up, but I was confident that I had made the best decision—or rather, I was following some good advice. This time, I didn't quit. The personal satisfaction and financial blessings as a result were simply amazing.

My career at UPS was full of ups and downs, but it turned out to be very satisfying and most rewarding. I met some of the hardest working people in the world and I value the many friendships made during my twenty seven years with them. I wouldn't trade even the worst of days with my friends and partners in that high pressure environment.

One of the most difficult weeks in my career came when the Teamsters went on strike in the late nineties. During those few weeks, I experienced some of the worst and best of the human condition. The worst occurred when we received word that one of our management team members had died in an accident not far from our district headquarters in Nashville. As soon as I heard the news, I quickly drove over to the scene of the accident where I met with our District Safety Manager on the closed off entrance ramp to I-65 near the rail yard. Unfortunately, the UPS tractor-trailer rig had flipped over the side of the ramp and landed about fifty feet below killing our Regional Safety Manager instantly. Strangely, the windshield of his tractor had popped out before going over the side and was laying there in front of us on the ramp. The District Safety Manager and I stood there alone; all the other emergency vehicles were down below at the point of impact. I asked him if he saw what I was looking at and he affirmed the hole on the driver side in the windshield. He told me he had already reported it to an officer. It was very disturbing because our vehicles had been hit by steel ball bearings and the hole staring us in the face was the size of one of them. We will probably never know on this side of eternity if one of those shots caused or contributed to the accident, but it did contribute greatly to the outrage our management team felt toward those responsible for many other cowardly acts committed by a few irresponsible people.

I began to feel genuine anger. I could not understand why a husband, a father, and a good partner lost his life so tragically in a no-win fight over power fueled by vindictiveness and greed. It was hard not to be judgmental. Our staff realized that type of violence did not represent the vast majority of the Teamsters, and neither did the vandalism that occurred later at our Clarksville center (receiving national attention), or the shots fired at one of our delivery vehicles, or the death threats, or the nails found in the tires of management's personal vehicles, including my truck. At times it was ugly to say the least, and I had to remind myself that most of these criminal acts were committed by only handful of people with evil intentions. The vast majority were good Teamsters standing up for what they believed to be a good cause. The really sad part was how both sides lost when it was finally over, and it had been at the expense of jobs and our customers. However, right in the middle of all the stress and turmoil came one of the most memorable answers to another prayer request for guidance.

My department was in charge of planning all of the day-to-day operations and our system was full of unsorted and undelivered packages after the work stoppage began. All available management were on deck each day to clean out the hubs and deliver a portion of the ground packages sitting at our delivery centers. We also continued to pick up and deliver air packages from our largest customers in an attempt to keep some of the air service in place.

There were far too many packages; progress to clean out the system was slow. Staff conference calls each day kept us abreast of negotiations, and we were somewhat optimistic in the beginning that the strike would not last long. However, that message began to change after the first week. On a Thursday afternoon, we were told it could drag on for a long time.

We were also told to start thinking about expanding our air operation and starting a small scale ground service, without employees of course. But just in case negotiations did improve, we also needed to be prepared to crank up the entire operation again—not an easy task when the system had been built for the efficient processing of about ten to twelve million packages per day. To further complicate matters, we had no idea which customers would return their business to us, and if they did, how much of a backlog there would be. Planes, pilots, tractors, trailers, and other equipment were out of place, and many details had to be worked out.

I had four managers working for me who were in charge of planning our huge tractor-trailer network, sorting facilities, air and delivery operations. All of them and their staff were personally driving routes delivering packages every day. The thought of planning for an expanded air and ground operation when we had not cleaned out what was already in the system, plus having a good plan ready in case the strike ended, was overwhelming. It was challenging enough to keep normal operations running smoothly. I knew our department did not have the capacity to do everything being asked of us. I'll never forget the depressed looks from the rest of the Division Managers as we left that Thursday afternoon conference call.

I went back to my office and sat silently at my desk, not knowing where to start. The offices were empty, because every available management person was out making deliveries. Then, faith began to well up in my heart as I began to pray. I remember thanking him for giving me that job. I also told him I knew he had always supplied what was needed to be successful as long as I put in my best effort. I then laid out three stacks of paper in front of me on my desk. They were my notes concerning each of the requests made by our regional and corporate offices. I told the Lord it was not possible given our staffing and time limitations to work out each plan adequately. I reminded him, as if he needed to know, there were a lot of people depending on our department to deliver a good plan at the right time, and I knew he had chosen me to lead that effort. I then concluded that I could only work on one plan and needed him to tell me which one.

I felt a surge of confidence at the end of that prayer because I knew from my experience as a seven year old that he existed (he was there with me) and that he was good (he wanted me to successfully carry out my responsibilities.) I had to leave the office early those afternoons, because it was too dangerous to exit the facility alone after sunset. But I was confident and comfortable knowing the Lord would answer.

That evening at home was very relaxing. My wife had prepared an especially tasty meal and I settled into bed with my Bible to read a few scriptures before nodding off. Normally, I did not rest well if I had a big project or an unsolved problem at work, but that night was different. When I came across Psalm 37, I knew I had my answer; the strike was going to end soon. Here are the portions that stood out to me from the first nine verses:

> "Do not fret because of evildoers, nor be envious of the workers of iniquity. For they shall soon be cut down like the grass, And wither as the green herb. Trust in the Lord, and do good: Dwell in the land, and feed on his faithfulness. Delight yourself also in the Lord, And he shall give you the desires of your heart. Commit your way to the Lord, Trust also in him, And he shall bring it to pass . . . Rest in the Lord, and wait patiently for him; Do not fret . . . because of the man who brings wicked schemes to pass. Cease from anger, and forsake wrath; do not fret . . . for evil doers shall be cut off; but those who wait on the Lord shall inherit the earth." (NKJV)

The following day I told the other Division Managers at the conference call that our department was going to start working on what we would do once the strike had ended. I did not mention the other two plans as I had no intention of wasting our time on them. I don't think anyone paid much attention to me because the news on the conference call wasn't good again; it appeared like this thing was going to continue for a long time.

After the call, I asked the District Manager if my guys could be excused from Saturday deliveries because we had some work to do. He gave me permission and later that day I bought a phone with a speaker and faxing capabilities for my home where I would conduct a conference call with my managers. I knew our planning meeting would last more than a few hours. I never told them anything other than we were going to work on plans to bring the entire system back up. That Saturday, we outlined what needed to be done.

On Sunday, I went to church as usual and my pastor asked me how things were going concerning the strike. He had been praying for me. I told him what the Lord had given me and I remember him nodding in agreement. The next day we returned to work and I kept our planners in the office to continue working on the plan. That evening our church held an elders meeting at my home, and before we started, one of them inquired about how things were coming along at work. I read the scriptures to them and told everyone that we were going back to work soon. They nodded in the affirmative as well, and we continued the meeting in our dining room.

When the meeting was over I'll never forget my son yelling out from the den as he watched the breaking news on the television: "Dad, you're going back to work; they just announced the strike is over!" The next day, our planners began to communicate the plan with the heads of each division and the execution went smoothly thanks to some great operators and a little guidance from above.

The Lord is so good. Even though life is difficult, and even though we will eventually succumb to death, I know that he will be with us every step along the way. I know he is also the One who will resurrect us, including our Regional Safety Manager. He promises to right all wrongs, reconcile and restore all relationships, and give us more than we ever lost in this life. From my experiences, from his Word, and from my vision, I know there is a greater purpose in all of the difficulties we face in this very short life. God is real. He is good. And even when things look bleak, he knows more than I do; therefore, I trust him.

During all those years the Lord answered many other prayers, showing his concern for me. Each answer increased my faith so that I could trust him in times like the one above. Some of the most important moments in my life took place during my time with UPS. These were faith-building memories worth hanging onto.

When I first came on board with the company, I was a part-timer and college sophomore. Later, I married and began full time work while still in school. I didn't make much money in the beginning and lived from paycheck to paycheck. I didn't mind because I'd never had any money and my main goal at the time was to finish my degree. No one warned me how hard that lifestyle would be because no one in our family had ever gone to college. The budget was tight and we could not afford much in the way of extras.

Growing up, I had been taught to give ten percent of my gross income to the church as a way of acknowledging his financial blessings upon me. Although I would learn much more about giving later in life, I lived out my convictions at the time, and tithed, even as poor as we were. But I also didn't have a problem asking him for financial help when the need became apparent. I never asked for extra money, only for what I needed. Amazingly, raises would come each time I prayed for one. Within the first year and a half, there were two occurrences of praying for an increase and receiving one that same week. At first, there was always the thought in the back of my mind that the timing of the increases could be coincidental, but after the third time, I was confident he was watching over me.

The last time I prayed for a little extra, a thought immediately jumped into my mind about solving a small problem at work. I really believed the Lord was telling me I would receive another increase after providing some help to one of the engineers. We had just leased a facility in Harlingen, Texas and it came with an above ground fuel tank. Each night we dipped a stick into the tank to determine the number of inches of fuel and that was to be converted to gallons remaining. Normally, tanks come with a chart, but no one knew where it was, so the task of developing one had been given to one of our engineers. I remember him asking me to look at his work as he tried to find a quick method for making all of the required calculations. I made a very unchristian-like and sarcastic remark about his erroneous approach, to which he replied appropriately, "Well, smart ass, then you solve it."

I knew how to do it and I took the problem with me to my physics lab class that night. I remember the cylinder was eighty-four inches in diameter and laying on its side. It was a simple calculus problem and I knew I could use integration to calculate the volume of fluid per inch. Curiously, my professor came over and asked me what I was working on while we had some dead time waiting for some lab results to come back. I explained and confessed it would take me a long time to do all of the calculations too. He got real excited about it and asked if he could take it home as he was learning computer programming and needed some practice. (The phrase "knock yourself out" wasn't around back then, but that is exactly what I was thinking.) I knew I would be too tired to get it done at home after a long fifteen hour day of work and college. The professor returned the next day with all eighty-four calculations done and I presented it to my boss the following day.

To summarize: I knew I needed more money to keep up with expenses. I knew the Lord would supply my needs. I knew the Lord had spoken to me about how to receive it. I knew he provided the assistance to get it done. I knew I had done what he required. Therefore, I knew the increase would be given on time. However, I was in total shock at the end of the week when my expectations were not met. This was a serious problem in my mind and I started praying that weekend and into the next week asking where I had gone wrong and why he was not speaking to me. My attitude was much like Kevin Costner in one of his last lines in the movie *Open Range* where he looked at his new wife and said something like: "Hun, if you don't do what I say, how's this marriage thing supposed to work?"

I wasn't angry; I was puzzled. As I continued in prayer I began to feel a certain peace about it. Two weeks later I reported to work on Monday morning with this gut feeling that he was going to answer my prayer that morning. The feeling was so strong and I remember becoming very nervous about how I would react in front of my boss. And then it happened. He called me to his office and asked me to close the door.

I kept my head down because I was having a hard time holding back the tears. When he told me I was receiving a raise retroactive to the week after I had finished the project, I could no longer hold it back. He must have thought I was a very unstable, or that he was the greatest boss in the world for making his employee so happy. The raise was a mere twenty five cents an hour, but it felt like a million bucks! At that moment I was once again completely overwhelmed by God's tender love and care. I plan to tell my boss the full story when I meet him on the other side. I was 21 years old at the time and I never asked God for more money again. I was convinced he would take care of me as long as I put in the effort and stayed in his will.

Before I eventually left UPS, I remember asking him if it was okay to leave. I mean, he had blessed me with more than I ever dreamed and I felt a tug to start writing some of the things he had taught me over the years. It seemed the longer I stayed at the company, the more responsibility I was given, which meant less time for what I really wanted to do. Additionally, the company began to change and we were asked to commit to impossible production increases without making the necessary process changes first. It was not in me to ask my managers to do more. Some of my closest friends and partners at the region and corporate offices gave me some good advice to do my best and not worry about the rest. After all, there were plenty of things to improve and if our district didn't meet the unrealistic goals, we wouldn't be the only ones. However, I felt it was time to hand those challenges to someone else . . . my UPS gas tank was running low. It was time for me to spend more time with my family and the pursuit of other lifelong goals. I wanted to write. Finally, one morning as I prayed during a trip to one of our operations in Paris, Tennessee, I felt his presence again, and I knew I'd been cleared for takeoff.

Three months after I left, our stock went public and tripled in value and I had a pile of it. Afterward, I received several calls from my former partners asking me how I knew the stock would take off like that. They felt I had inside information, or that I was one of the luckiest guys in the world. I've never regretted leaving, even though I could have stayed and possibly made a bigger pile. But I have lived in times of plenty and scarcity, and one thing I know for sure: while money is nice to have, it can't buy happiness. Happiness comes for me when I know he is near and I am serving and loving the ones that he loves.

So the Lord took care of me—and these stories are just a few of the many instances of his care and provision. But not only did he take care of my career, he also helped me with something far more important—choosing a wife and raising a family. After my first marital disaster, I knew I needed to finish my education and get a good job before taking on the responsibilities associated with being a good husband and father. It was a lonely first few years after the divorce, but I settled into a life of full-time college and part-time work. No longer carrying the responsibilities as a provider for anyone but me, it was still all I could handle. But I had some great times getting into motorcycling and traveling to new places between semesters.

Aside from a quick trip across the Red River so my uncle could buy some Oklahoma beer, I'd never been out of the State of Texas. So between semesters, a few friends and I went out west where we saw mountains for the first time, along with the vast expanse of the Painted Desert. We explored southern New Mexico in the Gila Bend area and later hiked to the bottom of the Grand Canyon. These were some of the best times of my life.

I also dated some girls from a local Bible college, but nothing ever developed. As time passed I began to wonder if I would ever marry again. I knew I had a few years left in college, and I wanted to meet the lady of my dreams sooner rather than later. More importantly, I needed to know if the Lord was still with me. One evening after feeling a bit sorry for myself, I told him I needed to know if he was still there . . . because I hadn't heard from him in a while. So, I asked him to find me a date by the next weekend as proof he was still listening. I told him I wasn't going to do anything but sit back and wait for someone to call me. In retrospect, it was a rather immature and faithless prayer, but I was hurting and lonely at the time and I knew he had no problem with me asking.

Friday night came and I had not received a call, so, I began fasting and praying. It was less about the date and more about how I was supposed to know I was on the right track without hearing from him occasionally. I finished my fast Sunday evening and went home to one of mom's great meals. I don't know how she knew, but after dinner, she asked me if I had been fasting. She told me the Lord would answer. Mentally and emotionally, I was spent, but I had a calmness and peace that the Lord knew exactly where I was and what I needed. Then, the phone rang. It was a girl named Melanie and she asked me if I wanted to see a movie with her that evening. I said yes with a smiling heart because the weekend was not yet over, and he had answered my simple prayer request, even if it was at the last moment. He seems to be predisposed to using drama as a teaching mechanism, usually showing up at the last moment! But when the drama is over, it's something you never forget.

You'd think I'd have been a little more relaxed after all of those answers to prayer, but armed with an invigorated faith that he was going to give me a wife . . . I became even more anxious! How nutty was that? A few months later, I drove out to my favorite prayer spot on a hill in Helotes, Texas. It had a peaceful westward view of the Texas Hill Country. I told the Lord I was tired of dating and waiting; I was ready to meet the woman I would marry. I did a little complaining too about the amount of time it was taking. I told him of my frustration and desire that he would hurry up and answer my prayer.

I drove down off that hill without an answer and decided to go see my older sister as I was lonely and there was no one else to talk to. After arriving at my sister's home, the person who she used as a baby sitter for her two sons answered the door. She was the first person I spoke to after coming off that hill, and I went inside and enjoyed the afternoon with my sister, my brother-in-law, and that baby sitter, who would later became my beloved wife. I didn't know it until much later that she had told my sister she was going to marry me the first time she laid eyes on me. As a typical male, I was a bit slow to catch on. For the next few months I dated a few others all the time complaining and wondering why the Lord had not answered. Looking back, it's kind of embarrassing since she had appeared right after my hilltop request.

After I graduated and landed an Industrial Engineering Supervisor position at UPS, we got married. This time I was better prepared to fulfill my role as a husband. As with any marriage, we've had our ups and downs, but she has been a great wife and mother to our children. While I worked long hours at UPS, she stayed at home raising our two kids and did an exceptional job, as evidenced by their character and success. We are so proud of them, and I'm so proud of my wife. She told me before we married that her main goal in life was to be a good mom, and she certainly achieved that dream.

These are just a few of the many stories of God's love and care for me over the years. I can't prove his existence with laboratory evidence, but I can say confidently that he loves and cares for me. That childhood vision served many purposes in my life, giving me hope and keeping me between the white lines on the roads of this life. But I always knew there was more. Much more.

3

BEHIND THE WATERFALL

~

For thirty three years I carried a heavy question in my mind about why I had been singled out to receive that great vision. But I had no hint of an answer. However, I had learned the Lord was with me during life's most critical moments, and this knowledge had given me considerable confidence that he would provide an answer at the right time. Strangely, I no longer felt the need to fast and pray as I usually did when stumped. I was okay with tossing up a few requests now and again asking for more information.

Meantime, attending church had become a very important part of my life. Growing up, our family attended non-denominational churches after leaving the Baptist organization. We ended up at Bethesda Temple with Dr. J.V. Foster as the pastor during my teenage years. He was highly independent and did not hold to many church traditions. There I learned that seeking the Lord meant I needed to read, study, ask and pray for his guidance. I read books on a variety of topics and became particularly fascinated with the topic of God's plan of salvation for all of humanity. I had so many questions and realized that what I was seeing in the scriptures was way outside the norm. One question would lead to another, and another, and I searched for answers until I was convinced one way or the other.

I received a lot of help along the way from JV, as everyone called him, who had some great insight on the subject. Not everyone who attended that church believed the way he did regarding God's plan for the ultimate reconciliation of all men, but it didn't seem to bother him, or stop him from teaching it—and a great teacher he was. In all my years I have never seen anyone, in any field, speak quite like him. If there was a man alive I could point to as being led by the Holy Spirit, I would choose him.

As an example, one Sunday morning he stopped in the middle of his sermon and pointed to my friend Jerry. Jerry was a few years older than me and I ran around with him and his younger brother for years. JV said God had just spoken to him and gave him these words for my buddy, "I'll be with you in the boat." JV said he had no idea what it meant, only that he was supposed to tell Jerry. Then, he went right back to his sermon. A few years later, Jerry, fresh out of high school, entered the Navy where he was assigned to submarine duty. A few years after that, I was at Jerry's home talking about his experiences and he showed me a signed letter of commendation from President Nixon hanging on his wall. Jerry's sub had been spying on the Russians in the Black Sea when they were spotted and subsequently bombed with depth charges from Russian destroyers. He also showed me a picture of the significant damage done to the sub. It must have been a very scary moment, but when the first charge went off, he remembered those words from JV, or rather from God, and was confident they would not be sunk. Incidentally, a submarine is referred to as a "boat" in the Navy. I don't know why, other than they are typically smaller than a ship. Whatever, God knew exactly what to call it.

Something similar happened to me during a Wednesday night sermon. JV stopped in the middle of another sermon and stepped quickly over the top of three pews, grabbed me by the arm and pulled me over the same pews to the front of the church in quite a dramatic fashion. He then had the church pray over me as he said God was calling me to teach. Later, I was told that my calling would be difficult and there were going to be many tears, but God would be with me. I already knew that last part.

Two years later I was sitting in a class in my senior year of high school when there was a call over the loudspeaker for me to come to the office. I remember some friends laughing thinking I was in trouble. I also remember the walk to the office trying to figure out what they knew and how they knew it. How had they learned about the day I skipped classes and went fishing? At the office the head counsellor met me and said she'd heard I wanted to be a teacher. I was relieved. I don't know where she got that idea from, but I said yes because of that Wednesday evening prophecy. She then had me fill out an application and I won a four year academic scholarship to study to be a teacher.

For most of my life I thought I was going to teach high school math or physics. Little did I know I would be teaching something far different. I should have figured it out; because for me, solving math and physics problems was enjoyable and never a source of frustration or tears.

I don't want to leave you with the wrong impression about our church; those types of prophecies at Bethesda Temple did not happen all the time. I'm sure some people were uncomfortable around it—I mean a man who hears from God? Of course, I was at home with it. I'm sure some visitors thought we were a bit crazy and a little on the wild side. However, as JV used to say, "Better to have a little wild fire than no fire at all."

Bethesda also had some intensely funny moments. During his sermons, JV had a habit of using people from the audience to help him teach. I always wanted to play the part of David, but never got that chance. Once he chose me and two other gentlemen of different ages to stand in front of the church to represent three righteous generations. I knew the other two elders chosen were wonderful Christian men, and probably the perfect example of genuinely good people. I think he chose me because I was the president of our Youth group at the time. I was proud to be counted among these guys—until JV started asking questions.

I guess he wanted to make a small point that he had chosen the right guys, so he began with the oldest and asked him three questions: "Do you smoke? Do you drink? Do you curse?"

Oh no! I knew what was coming and I didn't know what to say. I didn't smoke, and since it was basketball season, I hadn't snuck a beer in a while. So I knew I could honestly skirt the first two. But that last one . . . my friends and family in the audience knew about my temper when playing sports. They all knew what I would say about myself when I didn't play well. The words were never directed at any one else. I looked across the congregation and I could see the anxious looks on my friend's faces. They were no help, no help at all. What was I to do? Was I going to lie in front of family, friends . . . and God?

When it came my turn to answer, I boldly answered "no" to the first two. I still had no idea what to say on the third. And when he asked, it just came out of nowhere—"occasionally." At that moment there was instant relief in the church—laughter—and when JV finally gained his composure after nearly falling on the floor laughing so hard, he looked at the audience and said, "Well, at least he's honest," followed by another five minute round of comic relief at my expense. There was nowhere to hide. My mother always told me, "Be sure your sins will find you out." At that time I didn't know if that was scriptural, but nonetheless, I figured it was true. That was the most embarrassing moment of my young life.

Under JV's ministry, I learned the importance of Bible study with a concordance and other books that could be used to research subjects so I could come to my own conclusions. After a few years, the subject of universal salvation really began to grip my heart. I started believing the early church fathers had it right—that God would eventually reconcile all people. These men believed in judgment, but they just did not believe it would last forever. For them, the Bible taught the correction period would last as long as it took to bring the wicked to repentance. In other words, there would be no need for a finite being with limited knowledge to be held infinitely responsible, because an infinitely knowledgeable and merciful Father would eventually get through to them. The concept made sense to me, but I knew this was not in agreement with mainstream Christian thinking. I also knew there were so many translation errors and traditions to overcome that it would not be easy to convince anyone not open to new understanding. Life seemed to be difficult enough, and I found most people were seeking purpose, solace and comfort just to get through the day. Who needed more problems and controversy in their lives? I understood that perfectly. It is easier to go with the flow than swim against the tide of popular opinion and the status quo in any endeavor, whether in business, politics, or religion. However, I could not get this topic off my mind. I thought about it almost every day of my life since becoming aware of the issues at about twelve years of age. Little did I know the exposure to it would play such a significant role in my life. Was this the subject God was calling me to teach? Was this the one that would bring difficulty and tears?

I knew I was in the minority with my beliefs surrounding this subject, but for a time I believed logic and reason would eventually prevail if the subject ever came up for discussion with my Christian family and friends. When UPS moved me to the Dallas area, we attended a large nondenominational church for a time before moving over to a Baptist church. I stayed on the sidelines and kept my views to myself. In Salt Lake City, it was slightly different. There, we attended a much smaller church and made some great friends. When asked to teach the adult Sunday school classes and Bible studies, it was hard to remain silent. When pressed, I remember sharing my beliefs on this particular subject and the angry reaction it generated with some. I really didn't want to cause any conflicts, so we left that church after three years.

When UPS told me another move was in the works to a larger district, I prayed in earnest to be moved to a city where I could enjoy the fellowship of other like-minded Christians. I felt there was still much to learn, but in the seven years since leaving my hometown, there hadn't been anyone to have an intelligent, non-emotional discussion with about the subject. I knew there were other people out there like me; I just had to find them.

Upon moving to Nashville, I was excited and visited several churches but had no luck finding anyone with similar beliefs. My wife did find a small church and we fell in love with the people, atmosphere and the music. Once again, I was asked to teach Sunday school and Bible studies; I even had the privilege of standing in for the pastor a few Sunday mornings when he was out of town. Delivering a sermon that would be meaningful to all was one of the most difficult tasks I had ever been assigned, and I quickly realized I had not been called to serve in that capacity. I did serve as a deacon and an elder, and I was not nearly as uncomfortable, until I could no longer hide the passion I had for this subject. I don't need to go into details, but I was worried about the friction it might cause between the pastor and me as I understood his calling and his God given responsibilities. He had been taught that my way of thinking was a heresy and so he had to be very careful when confronting it. I could not stand the fact that I was causing him any difficulty. It was hard enough for him to run the church as we were struggling to keep the ministry alive, and he didn't need another headache. He was my friend, and I felt terrible about it all. However, speaking to him directly was not going to change a thing.

At the time, I was becoming more frustrated with my job at UPS. As responsibilities grew, that translated into more pressure, more time away from home, and less time for church and the passion for study of universal salvation. Finally, on a drive to one of our operations in Memphis, I could no longer contain my emotions. It was a three and a half hour drive from Nashville, which gave me plenty of time to tell the Lord exactly how I felt.

I told him that the move to Nashville seemed more like a big mistake and asked him why I was there. I asked him why I had not found a church with similar beliefs as I had requested several years earlier. I told him I seemed to be causing a lot of friction and making people angry wherever I went to church and how I did not want to be the source of so much stress for some of my Christian friends. I also told him I seemed to be obsessed with the subject and felt that maybe there was something wrong with me. I told him I knew I could be wrong, because I was only human and at the mercy of his direction. So, I let him know I was open to correction and would go back and apologize to everyone if he would just let me know the truth. And I meant it! I started thinking about each person I would have to make amends and what I would say to them. I told him I had no pride and nothing to lose, and it probably would be better anyway if I was wrong and all my friends were right. I told him I really didn't care anymore, one way or the other. All I wanted him to do was point me in the right direction.

I poured my heart out for about two hours talking to him just like he was sitting next to me in my car. And then, since I was on a roll, I threw in my final frustration—when was he ever going to tell me what that vision was all about? After thirty three years, I still had no clue. My frustration with life had reached an all-time high. Once again, I found myself in my car literally crying out with a loud voice for help and guidance. I was ready for correction and direction, and I couldn't have been any more sincere.

Evidently, the timing was right and he had brought me to that place where I was ready to receive. Within the next few minutes I had the answers to all of my questions except the one about why I had been moved to Nashville. That answer would come years later. I didn't hear any audible voices this time, but thoughts raced through my mind that caught me totally off guard.

First, he told me that I was not obsessed and the vision was all about what had become the passion of my life. However, he needed me to see it in his Word and experience his grace firsthand before he could explain the vision. I was shocked because that thought had never occurred to me. Then, several questions about the vision came to mind, and they were easily answered. After the first few, I knew the direction he was taking me.

The first question was, "What were you doing when I came to you?" Easy answer: "I was asleep."

"And what did I do next?" "You woke me up." Yes, he woke me up to his presence. That night he gave me the faith to believe in him. I received it without any effort on my part. If he hadn't awakened me, I'd be just as unconscious of his existence as any other person who hadn't been given faith yet.

The next questions centered on what I had done to deserve that most wonderful moment. Again, an easy answer: Nothing. Did I ask him to appear to me? No. Had I done anything great before or after the vision to

The Brightness around Him

deserve it? No. I was just your typical seven year old boy when he appeared to me. And my life afterwards was rather ordinary—and not always saintly.

So, I didn't ask for him to come, nor did I deserve it. I then realized Paul's experience on the road to Damascus was the same. He did not deserve it either, nor did he ask for it. God just decided to reveal himself to Paul making him an example for us to see the depth of his love for us. That is why Paul could write to the Church of Ephesus the following, which I will paraphrase from Ephesians 2:8–9 . . . "For by unmerited favor [grace] were you saved, through the process of believing [faith]. And the ability to believe [faith] is not self-generated, but a free gift. So that when everything is said and done, no man will be able to boast in his salvation," because it was God's work from the start to the finish. He really is the author and finisher of our faith.

The next question was, "What did I do next?" Easy answer: "You lifted me up off the hard-word floor and put me in a more comfortable place—a bed—a place of rest."

"Haven't you been telling everyone that My plan to reconcile everyone is the most comforting news you've ever heard?" Weren't those your exact words? Answer: "Yes!"

"What happened next?" Answer: "You opened my eyes and ears and showed me what you did on the cross." It was a visual display of his great love.

"So, I lifted you up, opened your eyes, and put you in a place of great comfort during your life." "Yes sir, I get it." I then started to realize the staggering implications behind that vision, not only for me, but for everybody on earth. The last thought was, "It is night-time and others now sleeping will be awakened to the same realization in the light of the morning."

Those few moments on that drive were just as exciting and as significant as his first visitation. That day I found a purpose in all those previous years of struggle. I already knew he existed and had an idea about his goodness, but now I really knew! It was explained in such simple terms—and I couldn't get over how great he was as a teacher.

The best instructors don't give their students immediate answers to every problem; rather they provide just enough information and guidance to allow the student to find solutions at their own pace. Looking back, he had led me to a point where all other solutions failed miserably on tests over language, logic, and love (and they still do to this day.) To me, thirty three years to work through a problem was tortoise slow, but the Teacher of teachers was patient enough and hung in there with me until I received what he wanted me to learn. Taking that much time to absorb it, and then finding out he was the One stimulating the interest and passion, was a very humbling thought.

This story was no longer about me and him; it was about him in me. I still did not know exactly what he wanted me to do with this revelation, but I began to relax a bit more knowing he was at the controls. It was a great relief; he had finally answered. Invigorated and recharged, if new questions emerged in the future, I felt more confident than ever that he would provide answers at the right time.

4

Gradual Understanding

~

I've come to believe the kiss of life exists in what we learn through experience. Knowledge gained through self-discovery is so satisfying and fulfilling that it quickly becomes a part of who we are. But most such discoveries require a lot of time and no small amount of pain. So just relaying a few stories without discussing some of the insight gained would leave this memoir less than complete. Without an increase in knowledge, storytelling becomes just another form of entertainment, and I want this book to be much more than that.

While writing this book, a friend asked me a very practical question: "What will be the take-away from your manuscript?" Well, one of my main goals is to leave readers with something useful. Obviously, to those with an atheistic or agnostic persuasion, my intention is to open your eyes to the reality of his presence so that you may begin, or resume, your personal journey of discovery with him. And for those who have already experienced God's love and care, my intention is to leave you with new insight into the richness of his kindness as perhaps you've never seen before. I've come to learn that embracing this perspective changes our focus from trying to "get people to heaven" to simply helping and encouraging each other as we travel along the way. Our mission will not only include offering hope through the good news of the Gospel, but it will also elevate acts of kindness, compassion and care to higher levels of priority than they might have been before. I believe that demonstrating God's love to a needy world is much more important than building attractive structures and programs in an attempt to secure something which our Father has already promised. It also will reduce our level of frustration as we place our confidence and trust in his ability to change the human heart.

These may appear to be lofty goals for a small book written by someone who is not a well-known author or spokesman for some denomination. But as I see it, all things are possible with him. I didn't write the story of my life; he did, and I believe it was written with a purpose in mind. I may have been slow to catch on, but as the greatest instructor in the universe, God has not failed in his efforts to teach me what he determined I should know and what I should pass along to you.

God is so good—much, *much* better than what is normally portrayed even by those who profess to know him. This is the real reason Jesus showed up in my bedroom that night—to destroy the darkness of preconceived notions about him by exposing the brightness of his goodness that surrounds him. The knowledge that he has gradually provided over the years eventually captured my heart and mind, and it is my desire to play a part as he captures yours in a way you may have never dreamed possible, for he really is that good.

I get excited when I start talking about what I have learned about his goodness. But before I begin telling you a little about what God led me to over the years, I need to ask for your patience as well as your ear for my writing pen has a tendency to over-do it. Remember, this is what I am so passionate about, and when I learned that I was not obsessed over this subject, but rather being motivated by the Creator of the universe, it gave me a tremendous amount of confidence and zeal. But I am also aware that not everyone shares the same degree of enthusiasm on this subject, and my family and friends have cautioned me about unnecessarily getting too far down in the weeds.

However, I feel like Tim (the Tool Man) Taylor from the sitcom *Home Improvement*. When he looked at a beautiful car, he was thinking more about what was under the hood—all that power and magnificent design. But the more utilitarian side of us doesn't really care all that much about mechanical intricacies; we are more concerned with practicality—like cost, reliability, and if we will look good driving it—nothing wrong with that. So, I'll try to hold back somewhat as I describe a little about what I found under the hood of this vehicle; just please try and remember the value proposition I submitted above—without an increase in knowledge, story-telling just becomes another form of entertainment. Also, keep in mind that God made me this way.

I'm going to start with a quick story, which tells a little more about how I am wired, and then use it metaphorically as an encouragement to launch your own investigation into his goodness. While serving as an Industrial Engineering Division Manager at UPS, each year I had to make a presentation to a special committee that approved investments in building and facility projects across the country. Each year every District I.E. Manager had to forecast business needs over the following ten years for each facility in their area of responsibility. If capacities were exceeded at any time, alternatives had to be evaluated and the best ones executed so service could be maintained. Alternatives might include small additions to a building, spinning off work to another facility, or replacing the building altogether. Cost was king and the company would not spend any money unless there was a significant return on investment, or there were no other reasonable alternatives to maintain service.

The committee members represented some of the brightest and most experienced minds in the company, and their wallets were tighter than a high pitched drum. Going before them was very stressful. There were over fifty districts throughout the company competing for the pool of available funds and the justification process seemed almost brutal at times. It had to be that way because the company needed to be sure it was investing its hard earned cash wisely.

My first area of responsibility was the state of Utah and most of Idaho. The first time I would present, I was the last one in our region to go before the committee. I wasn't too nervous this time around because I hadn't attended a meeting like it before and didn't realize how difficult it could be to get something approved, or how embarrassing it could be if I had not considered and put a cost to every reasonable alternative. At a later meeting, I remember being asked if I had gone to the business across the street and asked if they would move as we needed their property for expansion. That thought had never crossed my mind and I thought the project was dead at that point. The committee then entertained the idea of making an offer to our neighbor they couldn't refuse, and then finally dropped it in favor of my recommendation to end the lease and move to another location. However, they made this polite boy from south Texas feel kind of stupid for not discussing that alternative with the other company—"Hey, I know you boys have been here since the days of Brigham Young, but "this is the right place" for us, and we need you to move!" A Chief Operating Officer once

Gradual Understanding

called UPS a cross between the Marines and the Mormons; we could be righteously aggressive in our business practices at times.

Anyway, as I waited outside before it was my turn at bat, I remember the Regional I.E. Manager, Tyler, coming out during a break period warning me and another rookie, Danny, what to say and what not to say because the meeting was not going smoothly. We knew this was a big moment for us because we had been told that I.E. Managers were judged by two things that occurred each year—this meeting and how they did on an annual audit of their department. Danny, who was presenting for the Arizona District, kept us loose with his dry sense of humor. Our ignorance about the mood in the room and the volume of questions that were going to be fired at us worked in our favor to keep us calm. The following year both of us were better prepared and when a 4.5 earthquake hit while Danny was presenting, he told the committee that God was warning them to give him what he wanted or else he was going to bring the building down on them. I don't know if the humor worked in his favor that year, but laughter at this meeting was as out of place as matzo balls in clam chowder.

The committee took a small break after Danny presented, and I was told it had not gone particularly well for him either. There were about twenty five dark colored suits sitting around a u-shaped table arrangement as I entered the room. I knew many were from the northeast as I could tell from their accents, and when the lights were turned down for the overhead slides, it looked like a scene from a Mafia movie. The tension was almost visible and I was glad it wasn't my birthday. As I tried to present, I was immediately interrupted with questions and one very sarcastic remark from someone in the back of the room: "Well, the least you could do was tell us what page you are on." I had an orderly presentation for each project but they were jumping ahead trying to poke holes before I could adequately make my case.

At that point, Tyler stood up and told the group their questions might be answered if they would quit interrupting and let me finish. A quiet hush fell across the room and I finished with all the projects presented being approved. During the discussion about one of them, I remember someone in the room telling another to quit giving me a hard time and just approve the "damn thing." Whoever he was, I guess he held some sway. Afterwards, the gentleman apologized to me privately for the rude behavior of some during the meeting. He explained that some of the animosity had been a carryover from the night before where a board member and a vice president became verbally combative during happy hour. From his understanding, it was an on-going feud.

After that exposure, there were plenty of reasons for me to be more nervous about subsequent presentations and I always made sure I was armed with plenty of data to back up my claims. No stone would be left unturned because it was a matter of survival. I had to know every detail and I learned the value of knowing more about the project than anyone else in the room. It was a deadly strategy and in all my years of presenting, I only lost one project—but not really.

That year I presented seven projects and all were approved except the last one for Twin Falls, Idaho. I knew it was a borderline case and I didn't think the committee would approve it, but it was our intention to set it up for the following year. We also thought there was an outside chance they might give us the "damn thing" after wearing them down with six other very long and detailed project justifications. However, our Region Manager saw right through us. From the data he could see that the project could be delayed for a year and he interrupted me as I was finishing. Laughingly, he asked, "Jim, what are you doing? Are you trying to throw us a bone at the end?" After the meeting he came over and whispered in my ear, "Pitch Twin Falls next year and you'll get it." Our strategy worked, and the next year our opening pitch was a strike for Twin Falls.

But there was another project I presented just in front of that one. It was a relatively small one involving our Burley, Idaho center, and I knew there was some risk in moving forward with it too. We purposely placed it toward the end as well because the company did not usually address projects until the facilities had outgrown their physical capacities. Burley was more of a cosmetic issue. It was a tiny center located near the Snake River and the facility consisted of an old forty foot Coca Cola trailer, or maybe it was a Pepsi trailer; I can't remember. It had four doors on each side and we used them to load our package cars each morning. Another door on one end was required for unloading the inbound trailer that arrived each morning. Our sophisticated conveyor system used to sort and load the packages into our delivery trucks consisted of a set of rollers running down the middle of the trailer (this is where you are supposed to laugh.) We knew the trailer's original owner because the words were bleeding through what appeared to be a cheap one-coat-paint-job. Additionally, the entire trailer was leaning heavily toward the river as it slowly settled into ground that was once part of the river bed. It leaned so much that packages being unloaded onto the

Gradual Understanding

middle section of rollers would often fall to the floor of the trailer unless someone was standing there to catch them.

That's what I came to love about UPS; literally, they would not spend a penny until they absolutely had to. One year I received a call from our corporate offices in Greenwich, Connecticut. They had one question and one directive. They wanted to know how many facilities did not have a restroom and then told me to quickly put together a ten year plan for each that included a place "to go." A few days prior, a student worker at one of our small centers in southern Utah apparently needed to take care of some personal business and did so in a nearby field. When some lady looked out her back window and observed the act of nature, the local police were immediately called.

The next day, the headlines in the local newspaper read, "UPS—No Place To Go!" Of course, that made the evening news too as there was not much to report about in the State of Utah on a daily basis. The following morning, some local news reporters showed up with their cameras and interviewed one of our drivers. When asked where they used the restroom, the driver humorously replied as he pointed, "In that dumpster." How perfect! When I heard him, I laughed so hard I had tears in my eyes. However, our corporate headquarters didn't think it was so funny, and those were the only projects I ever presented that were approved without any resistance. I guess you could say we flushed out our problems and dumped those facilities which had made us the butt end of jokes in the news. Yes, I know that was not nearly as clever as the line of the year, "In that dumpster!"

When presenting the Burley project, I knew I had to lean on emotions rather than on trying to justify the need for change with numbers and a positive ROI (Return On Investment). I wrote out my speech and was prepared to the hilt to defend our position. As I started the presentation, we put up a picture of the facility on the overhead screen. I could hear laughter in the back of the room along with some mumbling as I began my pitch. After a few more moments, I heard my name being called by the Regional Manager. "Jim... Jiiiim... Jim! You can stop now, Jim." I looked up and he was laughing along with the other decision makers. "You got the project; move on."

I remember not knowing what to say or do next because I had so much more material to cover, and well, I wanted to give it to them. I wanted to share every bit of information I had worked and worried over for weeks. I was ready to answer questions; I was ready to plead my case with facts and figures; I was ready to defend as I had done multiple times before. But all of my research and pain in building a case for a new facility was no longer needed. The picture had done the job. But I was lost. To this day, I still want to go back and finish.

Now, with that insight into my personality and my sometimes unnecessary desire to drive home a point with everything I've learned about a particular subject, I hope you can be patient with me as I discuss what I'm really passionate about! I blame these tendencies on UPS and God; they drove me to it . . . in a UPS package car!

After that long introduction, I'm going to draw two mental pictures of two different religious human sorting systems that in my opinion have seen their better days and are in dire need of replacement. I will follow that up with a third picture to illustrate a better solution. To do that, I offer below a short article I wrote recently that was published in Clyde Pilkington's Bible Student's Notebook, a free weekly newsletter I highly recommend. I hope the first two views on our imaginary overhead will expose some of the known defects and give you reasons to consider a much more efficient replacement model. I hope you will also see how the message on the side of the first two facilities does not represent who we really are and no attempt at covering over them with a cheap coat of paint can hide it from the rest of the world. My article:

THREE VIEWS OF GOD'S VICTORY

Religion is a very emotional topic, and it should not be surprising that there are different interpretations of scripture on the topic of eternity as we humans attempt to describe what we see when staring through that dark glass that Paul referred to in 1 Cor 13:12. Since it is such a hot topic, it might be best if we remind ourselves up front that his plan is not dependent on our knowledge, or lack thereof, and that focusing on the things we have in common occasionally, might keep the conversation more respectful of the wonderful customized training he is providing for each of us. I believe that each individual is a work-in-progress. So, before I provide some of what I have learned in what follows, my hope is that it will be helpful to all and disrespectful to none. Please forgive me in advance if in my exuberance, I stray.

I'd like to start with what we have in common, namely, God is love, and according to scripture, love never fails. Never! But confusion abounds in our different predictions about how love's victory will be achieved and what the end

Gradual Understanding

product will look like. Boiled down, the Christian church offers three different pictures of what an ultimate win for love, our Father's final victory, will look like. The question is, which one is right?

In the first image, some see many celebrating in heaven while others suffer in hell-fire and brimstone—forever—tormented day and night with no possibility of escape. And despite the availability of an endless amount of time to consider the terrible mistakes made during their finite time on earth, there's no possibility of parole for the once wicked, no possibility for a change of heart, and even if there were, the time for extending mercy and forgiveness has long since passed. And even though all wrongs have been made right in heaven, and even though all that was lost in a previous life has been restored, and even though restitution has been made beyond all expectations and beyond our wildest imagination with the redeemed enjoying all of it for billions upon billions of years, in spite of all of this, the possibility of a change of heart and reconciliation for God's wayward sons and daughters is gone. God tried to reach them during the few years they had on earth. He tried really, really hard, and now, hell is a permanent reminder of that colossal failure.

I personally witnessed one of America's favorite pastors justify this picture of victory when he said that God was a gentleman and would not force his will on anyone, but rather he was just honoring their request to choose hell over heaven. And the good man made that statement right after he spoke about his understanding of the parable of the rich man in Hades trying to warn his brothers—"Don't come here!" It did not sound to me like the rich man wanted to be there.

Regarding free will, how ironic it is for men to say he won't violate man's free will but these same men have no problem believing that God will one day force all men to bow and confess to Christ, then keep them in a place they'd rather not be for all eternity. Furthermore, retired philosophy professor Thomas Talbott demonstrated the lack of logic in this assertion when he compared it to a child sticking his hand in an open flame. Children do some stupid things in spite of our warnings, and sometimes, they get burnt. But if they were to continue to stick their hand in the fire every time they saw an open flame, wouldn't that qualify as insanity? And wouldn't we seek professional help for such a child? Certainly, we would not condemn them. Writing off your children as people who will never learn, is that a picture of a parent's love that endures all things and never fails?

In the second image of God's victory some see many celebrating in heaven while others who after being raised from the dead and judged for their bad behavior, are then annihilated and never to be heard from again. The end result is much the same as in the first view, but rather than erecting a permanent monument of his failure, God decided to wipe them out. I understand that a recent Pope was against the death penalty because he thought that with a little more time, the guilty just might repent. But in this second picture, just as in the first, God decided against allowing any more time for repentance.

Personally, I don't really understand why the dead would need to be taken from the graves just to be sent right back. Maybe we need them to suffer death one last time to make sure we get even with them? This may satisfy our need for justice because these people should get what they deserve, by god. I'm just glad the rest of us don't receive what we deserve.

To the family and friends in heaven of those exterminated, how do we find them reacting to the idea of never seeing their loved ones again? I heard another pastor of a mega church explain how people in heaven will be able to overcome the sadness of lost loved ones annihilated or suffering throughout eternity. The title of his message was displayed in flashing bright lights outside the church. The sign read "Hell Yes!" "Heaven will be like eating a nice big juicy steak," the pastor explained. "While enjoying it, you are not thinking about the starving people all over the world. That's what heaven will be like." I noticed a quiet hush fell over the building...

And that brings us to the third picture of God's ultimate victory—everyone celebrating in heaven with some arriving sooner than others, but all eventually getting there after having been salted with fire, because the scripture says that everyone will be salted with fire, after having been judged for their deeds and forgiven of their sins once recognizing their own human frailty and the need for a change of heart, and after having acknowledged what Jesus provided for them by his death on the cross. It took a little more time for some, and maybe a lot more time for the really rebellious, but eventually they finally came in because love endures all things and never fails. A brilliant Creator foreordained the end, and now we look back and see how he used free will as an instrument in his hand. As Talbott pointed out, the more we rebelled against God, the more miserable and tormented we eventually became, giving us even more incentive to repent. The consequences of sin ended up being a means to reveal what happens when we don't act in love towards each other.

People who see this picture believe that all paths have the same destination—reconciliation to him and each other. In this picture, Christ has become all in all, not all in some. Every tear has been wiped away off all faces, not just some, and every family and nation has been blessed, not just a few, because Jesus

Gradual Understanding

became the Savior of the world, not just the Savior of some, when he took away the sins of the world, and not just some, by drawing or dragging all men to him, not just some, and now there is no more death because of his victory over the grave.

A few brief words on church history will help us understand how each point of view came to us. About the turn of the fifth century, Jerome wrote the Latin Vulgate to bring unity to the Latin church. Many different Latin dialects led to many different translations of the Bible, and this was causing confusion. Jerome's version pulled everyone together and his translation became the Bible for the next 1,100 years.

In the process, Jerome had some difficulty translating into Latin the Greek word *aion* in its noun and adjective forms. *Aion* is where we get the English word, eon. However, he was clear in his belief that the words meant age and age-lasting. Another very influential man at the time, Augustine, argued with Jerome that the words meant eternity and everlasting, even though he knew nothing about the Greek language and actually said that he hated it. Jerome was a follower of many of the early church fathers who did believe in the reconciliation of all things – men like St. Clement of Alexandria, Origen, Gregory of Nyssa, Ambrose of Milan, and Basil of Caesarea. These men wrote, spoke and taught the Greek language. They believed that *aion* meant age, and that punishment was remedial and restorative in nature. Incidentally, I know of ten other Greek words that do mean unending, but none of them are ever used in connection with punishment in the Bible. These men did believe in punishment for the wicked, but in their view, such punishment will not last forever. Once it accomplished its purpose, there will be no need for it any more.

Later, the Latin church dominated Europe and Augustine's view of eternity as in the first picture above, was adopted by most. Augustine believed that the majority of mankind was "one damned batch of perdition." He believed that:

1. God was sovereign and his will would be done.
2. The majority of mankind was predestined for eternal torture.
3. Since most would miss Heaven, God did not want all to be saved.

Augustine's philosophy became the forerunner to Calvinism. Later, Jakobus Arminius came along and tried to correct this rather harsh view of our Heavenly Father with his belief that:

1. God does want all men to be saved.
2. Most of mankind will still miss heaven as in Augustine's view.

3. Therefore, God's will will not be done.

Those holding the first two views believe that all things said about our Heavenly Father in the Lord's Prayer are true, except one. Is he our Father? Is he in heaven? Is his name holy? Will his kingdom come? Will he give us our daily bread? Will he forgive us? Will he lead us not into temptation? Will he deliver us from the evil one? Is the kingdom his? Is the power his? Is the glory his? But somehow, in the middle of all these strong affirmations that Jesus commanded us to pray in faith believing, his will is not done on earth as it is in heaven. That's a very sad outcome, and a very sad statement about God's ultimate victory, if that is indeed the end result.

And another sad statement in history, in my opinion, came from King James after ordering the translation of scripture into English, when he told those working on the project that whatever they did, they should not upset the orthodoxy of the church. So, Augustine's paradigm and his biases became embedded in the King James Version (KJV) and then in our modern translations, and most sadly, the majority of Christians are not even aware this happened.

Those early church fathers who saw the third picture of love's victory believed that:

1. God was sovereign and his will would be done.
2. God wants all men to be saved.
3. Therefore, our Father loses none, because love never fails.

So there you have three pictures of what God's victory might look like and a little history behind them. Of course, by now you know my opinion. Simply put, I have no doubt God desires to save all men. And furthermore, I believe he has the ability to pull it off. I love this quote from Martin Luther (1483–1546): "God forbid that I should limit the time of acquiring faith to the present life. In the depth of the Divine mercy there may be opportunity to win it in the future."

I understand some of the reasons for differences of opinion given the rather threatening descriptions of punishment found in some of our best-selling translations of the Bible. Words like eternal, damnation, hell, the lake of fire and brimstone and the second death sound very convincing. However, I also know the history behind these words. Some of them are not even found in the original Hebrew and Greek language, while others, like the second death found in the Book of Revelation, are not to be taken literally

Gradual Understanding

any more than there will be a literal pregnant woman clothed with the sun and the moon under her feet wearing a crown of twelve stars, or will there ever be a literal lamb that will speak like a dragon (will she speak with a deep voice like Smaug?), or a woman who will ride a literal scarlet colored beast having seven heads and ten horns, (although this closely resembles the missus when I miss trash day) or will Babylon cause all nations to literally drink wine from the literal wrath of her fornication, because wine comes from grapes, not wrath (a little applause for the insertion of literary humor please) or will whole nations literally fornicate with a harlot (although that might garner some interest)?

I also know hundreds of other scriptures that cannot be explained by those holding the first two views. There is so much to discuss here and I genuinely wish I could unload all I have discovered in a few pages so you could have all of the facts to make your own determination. I feel the need to do this because it is rarely conveyed from the pulpits of our churches. However, I promised not to go too far down into the weeds, so I will only give you a few examples of some of the misinformation that has made its way into some of our modern translations and into the minds of many good Christians trying to keep the human packages from falling off the rollers as they are sorted for their final destination.

I've already briefly mentioned the controversy surrounding words translated as eternal and everlasting and I'll have more to say about them later. But what about other frightful words mentioned in the scripture? What about the word, "damnation"? Did you know this word was invented by a Latin lawyer named Tertullian about two hundred years after the time of Christ? The term has been useful for many of us Dallas Cowboy football fans, especially toward the end of the past few seasons, but it seems entirely out of place when used to describe a loving God's end game plan for most of his creation. (Incidentally, being a Cowboy fan can be a religious experience for they are the only team I know that can make 100,000 Texans stand up and yell the name of our Lord and Savior at the same time.) Seriously, here's what my friend Mike wrote about damnation:

> "There probably isn't a scarier word in English than this word. When you look for damnation in the King James—sometimes call the Authorized—Version of the Bible, you will find it occurs eleven times, yet there is no word in the Greek New Testament's vocabulary whose fundamental meaning is damnation. In all eleven cases (Matt 23:14; Matt 23:33; Mark 3:29; Mark 12:40; Luke 20:47; John 5:29; Romans 3:8; Romans 13:12; 1 Cor 11:29; 1 Tim

5:12; 2 Peter 2:3) the Greek word translated "damnation" comes from either #2917 (*krima*) or #2920 (*krisis*) in *Strong's Concise Dictionary of the Words in the Greek Testament* . . . and both of these words have the fundamental meaning of decision, judge, or judgment. With that information, we ask the reader to consider the following questions:

1. Out of the seventy-five verses where *krima* or *krisis* are used, why were only eleven of them chosen to be translated with the word damnation?
2. Why weren't all of them translated as damnation? (because the make-believe charade would not have made sense in the other sixty-four)
3. Since these words have the fundamental meaning of decision or judgment, what prompted Tertullian to introduce damnation into the Latin version?"

Mike and I submit the answer to that last question may be found in Tertullian's failure to see God as anyone other than a judge. That he is, however, we'd also like to add that he is a merciful Father as well. Tertullian did not know Greek and unfortunately, he made many other mistakes by inventing and inserting several other words that are nowhere to be found in the original language of the scriptures.

Continuing with other language and logic issues that confronted me during my research, let's take the word "hell." Another friend, Gary Amirault, neatly compiled some additional questions and I've added a few of them to our list for consideration.

If eternal damnation in hell is a reality, and so vitally important, why didn't God make that warning plain right from the beginning? For something so critical, why didn't he warn Adam and Eve right out of the gate? All we can find is God's warning that the penalty for eating of the tree was death, not eternal life in fire and brimstone.

1. Does Matthew 25 teach we will be sent to hell for not feeding the hungry or visiting the sick? There is not one mention in this entire passage that "belief in Jesus is what differentiates the sheep from the goats.
2. If eternal hell is real, why didn't the Apostle Paul (who was commissioned to preach to the nations) warn anyone of it in any of his letters? Better yet, why didn't he warn them repeatedly? Didn't Paul say in Acts 20:27 he had declared the entire counsel of God?

Gradual Understanding

3. If eternal hell is real, why isn't hell mentioned even once in the book of Acts in any of the evangelistic sermons that were recorded by the early apostles? As a matter of fact, hell as a translation of Hades or Gehenna does not appear in any of the Epistles! Paul never uses Gehenna, and his only reference to Hades was in celebration of its defeat! Only 2 Peter 2:4 mentions a place called "tartaros" as a temporary holding place for fallen angels.

In summary, thirty-one references to hell in the Old Testament KJV are all translations of Sheol, meaning "the grave." Those have been corrected in most modern translations. In the KJV, of the twenty-four times hell is mentioned in the New Testament, ten come from the translation of Hades, which is the Greek word for Sheol, the grave, thirteen come from Gehenna, a reference to the garbage dump outside of Jerusalem, and one from tartaros.

Another interesting study can be done on the lake of fire and brimstone found in Revelation 21:8. Since the text was written in Greek, let's see how the Greeks understood these terms. Brimstone is sulfur, something sacred to the Greeks. It was used to purify, cleanse, and to consecrate for divine service. The root word in the Greek is *theion*. The root *theo* means God. *Theou* means "to hallow, make divine, or dedicate to God." For verification, check out this web page for a company that mines sulfur: http://www.georgiagulfsulfur.com/history.htm.

So what is the Lake of Fire? Here is what I discovered the early church believed it to be: The fire was spiritual and was to be applied in one of two stages, this life, or the next. Those who wished to avoid the second must be willing to submit to the first. Here are a few quotes from some of the early church fathers: Clement of Alexandria (150–213 AD): "Fire is conceived as a benefit and strong power, destroying what is base, preserving what is good; therefore, this fire is called 'wise' by the prophets." He further described this fire as "saving and disciplinary, leading to conversion." Origen (180–253 AD): "As therefore we say God is a consuming fire, what is it that is to be consumed by him? We say it is wickedness, and whatever proceeds from it, such as figuratively called 'wood, hay and stubble' which denote the evil works of man. Our God is a consuming fire in this sense; and he shall come as a refiner's fire to purify rational nature from the alloy of wickedness and other impure matter which has adulterated the intellectual gold and silver; consuming whatever evil is mixed in all the soul." Bishop Titus of Bostra: "The punishments of God are holy, as they are remedial and salutary in their effect upon transgressors; for they are inflicted, not to preserve their wickedness, but to make them cease from their sins. The abyss . . . is indeed the place of punishment, but it is not endless. The anguish of their sufferings compels them to break off from their sins."

This brings us to language concerning the second death. Revelation 20:10–15 says on judgment day those whose names were not found in the book of life are to be cast into the lake of fire, which is the second death. The first view holds that the lake of fire is literal, and the second death is symbolic; otherwise, how could a person be tortured forever if they were not alive to feel it? The second view holds that the lake of fire is symbolic, but the second death is literal. This view does not seem possible, for in verse ten we find the devil, the beast, and the false prophet being tormented day and night forever and ever, according to their interpretation, after having been tossed in the lake. The scripture is emphatic that the lake of fire is the second death. So how can their torment be without end if those thrown into it die?

The third view believes both to be symbolic. The Book of Revelation begins with a stated purpose: "The revelation of Jesus Christ," which "he sent and signified by his angel to his servant John." To signify means to make known by signs or words. And a sign is any symbol that represents an idea. Being in the third group, it is difficult for me to switch to a partial literal interpretation at the end of chapter twenty after nineteen plus chapters of symbol after symbol and metaphor after metaphor. With the understanding that the lake of fire is part of a purification process that lasts for a finite but unknown period of time, it only makes sense that it is like a second death because those dunked in it are forever changed. What happened to Saul on the road to Damascus is the perfect example of the transformation that occurs after having been three days in the lake of fire. Afterwards, Saul was given a new name and a new purpose, and his life and character were forever changed. I bet we won't find Saul's name in the book of life, but I bet we *will* find Paul's.

My only purpose in this chapter is to introduce some of what was lighting-my-fire all those years and still does, so to speak. I hope it will stimulate further research on your part. As a start, you may want to consider going to Gary Amirault's web page found at tentmaker.org and read some of the testimonials of other Christians, including several ministers who changed their minds after a little investigation of their own.

One amazing testimony came from a minister named, G.A. Roach:

Gradual Understanding

> One day as I was preparing my Sunday message, I had a crisis. The passage for that week's message was Romans 5:18. Romans and Ephesians are my two favorite books in the New Testament. My favorite chapters are Romans 5 and 8. But that day, when I read Romans 5:12–21, it was as if I had never before seen that passage. I read and re-read the passage. The more I read, the more convinced I was that I was misunderstanding what Paul was writing. After all, I earned a Master of Divinity and Doctor of Ministry (Preaching/Biblical Studies) from Southwestern Baptist Theological Seminary. I knew what Paul taught! I went ahead and prepared a message on the passage in Romans 5. But I resolved to study this out and 'prove' that Paul could not possibly be teaching that all will be made alive.
>
> I spent a year in study, with a prejudice against the theology that all will be saved. I did not want to rush into anything that might be a heresy. However, to my consternation (and later relief), the more I studied, the more convinced I became that God did indeed reconcile the world to himself; that all are made alive through one act of righteousness; and that God would eventually bring all men to himself.

Later in the testimonial he tells of beginning to teach this to his congregation and how they accepted it along with the congregation of a second church that he has pastored. Other testimonials from ministers to worship leaders and lay people are also shared at this site.

One of the most impressive testimonies I have ever read about is found in the book *Spiritual Terrorism* by minister and counselor, Boyd Purcell, PhD. I read all 474 pages in one weekend as I could not put the book down. It is an easy read and his story about leaving the first two views for the third is fascinating.

In this chapter I have given you a tiny bit of insight into what I gradually came to understand over these years. Before we close it out, I want to ask two questions to those who want to continue to sort souls from that old burley trailer platform (that was another attempt at humor) or the new replacement model. We know that Jesus paid the debt for all sins; I mean he paid the debt—all of it. In other words, there is no more debt for sin . . . because he paid the note off. I want to be sure we all have the right understanding: in God's eyes, there is no more debt. And now with the debt fully paid off by the sacrifice of his Son Jesus, God has the right to be kind, if he wants to be kind. He doesn't have to be kind, but let's say he decided to be kind. In that case, if he did bring others to repentance at some point in the future, and afterwards extended mercy to them (including those who have done wrong to you and me):

1. Will we be offended?
2. Why, or why not?

I think these questions may be helpful in making sure our hearts are right, no matter which view we hold, and that we are not merely seeking vengeance. That's our Father's job: "Vengeance is mine; I will repay, says the Lord." Romans 12:19.

Speaking of repayment, look at what justice required for victims of crimes under God's laws as given to Moses—victims were to be repaid by the guilty for their losses. However, as in the case of death, some wrongs could never be made right by the guilty. This is where our Father steps in, for he is the only One who can make things right and restore what seems to be forever lost. He promises, "I will repay (your debt)." And to add icing on the cake, he promises to restore what we have lost by the sins of others. Again, "I will repay (your losses)." In the long run, he's got us covered on both ends of the law—what a great Father!

5

COUNTING CLOUDS

Another few years would pass after the road to Memphis experience before I would receive another significant insight. During that time I waited on the Lord for guidance, and it wasn't easy. Unless asked, I made every effort to hold back my passion for this topic, believing the Lord would give me opportunities to teach at the right time. I did not want to cause trouble, especially among my church friends, and no one was asking about it anyway. I took that to mean most were either comfortable with standard explanations, too busy to bother with the controversy, or lacked the confidence to question obvious inconsistencies. As a friend who grew up in the northeast pointed out to me, we southerners tend to erroneously consider directness as rude. That makes us uncomfortable with telling it like it is. We'd rather dance around and avoid confrontation.

Toward the end of that period, I was invited to a men's Bible study at our church. Honestly, I was hesitant to go because it was held early on a weekday morning and I felt I really didn't have time for it because of my job at UPS. I was also worried about the subject of my passion coming up and the friction it might cause if I said anything about it. However, the desire to develop friendships at church overcame the perceived obstacles, and I decided to join in. My friend Terry was leading a study on Ephesians, and they had already gone through most of the first chapter when I came for the first time.

It was a great group of well educated, highly intelligent and very successful Christian men. I got along well with each one and felt I could learn from them given their experience and expertise in the Word. However, the night before I told the Lord in prayer that if the topic of his grace were to come up, I was not planning on saying anything. I just wanted to be a sponge, get along with everyone, and not make any waves.

Before dozing off to sleep, I decided to read ahead in Ephesians in case there was a question and answer period at the beginning. I did not want to look like a fool; these guys were knowledgeable and sharp! When I arrived at chapter two, verse seven, I began to see something I had never noticed before. Given what I had previously learned over the years, it was simply awesome. I couldn't sleep as my mind raced with the implications. I remember looking at the clock beside my bed, which said it was 2:30 a.m., and I knew I had to get up at 5:30 a.m. The thought of another high pressure eleven hour day at work on top of the Bible study generated some anxiety. I thanked the Lord for what he had shown me and asked him to leave me alone as I needed some sleep—just kidding! But I did remind him that I needed some rest.

I went to the Bible study and thankfully there were no questions at the beginning because my mind was deader than a high school student in algebra class . . . on a Friday . . . after lunch. Everything was going well until we came upon chapter two verse eight. After reading it Terry stopped and told the men that he always had trouble with that scripture because it didn't fit his paradigm. He then asked if anyone was experiencing the same degree of difficulty.

I dropped my head and began a hurried and almost desperate prayer. I reminded the Lord of the previous night's prayer when I said I would refrain from speaking about this subject. I then raised my head slightly and everyone I could see around me had their hands raised in acknowledgment of the problem, except me. I quickly dropped my head again and continued to pray. My good friend, the pastor, then commented that it had always bothered him too.

At that point, I felt Terry staring at the top of my head while he asked if anyone had any insight. That confounded Tertullian word came to mind, but I knew the Lord was going to speak to this group, and since 2nd Century church father Tertullian wasn't with us that morning, I was probably the vessel he would use. I thought about his kindness and concern for me and my friends and knew this was a special moment, if only I could find the right words. I took a deep breath and asked one last time for his help before responding.

With what I had learned the previous night in verse seven, and all of my previous experiences, I began my "presentation." I told my friends I'd been up most of the night, having found something in this passage of scripture that might be helpful.

Counting Clouds

My opening premise was this: that the Holy Spirit was speaking through Paul to a bunch of Ephesian believers, who were just like us. What I knew about Ephesus, but didn't spell out that morning, is that of the six major schools of Christian learning in the first few centuries after Christ, Ephesus alone was where conditional immortality was taught—the eventual annihilation of the wicked, the second picture/view of love's final victory. In contrast, Carthage, where the Latin language was dominant, they taught eternal torment in hell for non-believers. And the other four Greek-speaking schools taught the eventual salvation of all men. I also knew from a previous Barna survey that most Christians today believe like the Ephesians did.

This exciting realization was part of what had kept me up the previous night. I thought, how perfect! In speaking to the Church at Ephesus, the Lord was also speaking to believers today, to me and my friends. He is acutely aware of our blind spots and promises to open our eyes at the right time.

I started in verse seven with a key phrase, "In the ages to come." I admitted to my friends that I had missed the significance of this phrase many times, until the previous night when I came to realize it meant "the future." Duh. There were a couple of chuckles. From the next phrase, "he might show," I concluded that if he had to show us something in the future, we must not understand it right now; hence, our questions about verse eight. It was as if the Holy Spirit were saying, "I know you boys are going to really struggle with this one, and I promise to clear it all up at some point in the future." And since he knew back then about the confusion, and he had plenty of time to put a halt to it, but did not, I also had to conclude it was part of the training package.

My thoughts were racing. I didn't want to get ahead of myself, but I thought about how many centuries and how much infighting it took before The Reformation brought the church an understanding that the grace of Jesus has supplied our righteous—that we are not saved by works. And I believe the church is now in the middle of a second major struggle over the second part of salvation's equation—Jesus not only supplies the righteousness we need, but he also has elected to supply the faith we need too. The implications are mind-boggling to someone stuck in Augustine's paradigm. This is why my buddies were struggling with verse eight, because they hadn't yet realized the richness of his generosity! But I didn't mention any of these things that morning.

What I *did* ask them was what it could possibly be that God might need to show us in the future because of our lack of understanding now. The answer is found in the next phrase—"the exceeding riches of his grace in his kindness toward us in Christ Jesus." The Holy Spirit is saying God's kindness will exceed the expectations even of believers.

And why is it that our expectations are far too low? That answer is found in the words that follow. "For" is a conjunctive word linking the previous statement and could have easily been translated as "because." His kindness will exceed our expectation because many in our Christian family have not yet recognized the *Blue's Clue* in verse eight: faith is an unmerited gift given, and not merely offered. If it were offered, some could brag that they received it while other big dummies did not. The truth is that God gives us the faith to believe even if we weren't looking for it. No man is going to be able to boast in anything he did to achieve his salvation; for we are "his workmanship." (For those who never saw the Nickelodeon™ TV series from 1996–2007, *Blue's Clues,* Blue was a puppy who placed her paw prints on three clues. The star of the show, Steve, had to deduce from the clues, with the help of off-screen children, what Blue wanted to do. It was a big hit with kids, and even some adults.)

At that point, I wished I could have helped with another Blue's clue— when Jesus compared Spiritual birth to physical birth in a conversation with Nicodemus. No human was given a choice to be born or not. However, I could not give that clue because the Lord's analogy had not yet sunk in. How could I have missed it?

I then pointed my friends toward the man who wrote those words in Ephesians—Paul. He was the perfect example of God's grace exceeding the expectations of men; even believers in Paul's day were skeptical at first. God had taken an enemy, someone who was not seeking Christ, but rather participating in the deaths of other believers, and he dropped faith in Paul's heart and made him his chief apostle and one who would write about half of the New Testament. Is it any wonder Paul wrote that the faith to believe is a gift from God? (For an enlightening book about how we are saved and justified by the faith of Jesus, not by self-generated faith in Jesus, I strongly recommend Caleb Miller's *The Divine Reversal*. It is outstanding!)

Next, I briefly addressed the translation of the Greek word *aion*—an age—the New Testament noun whose fundamental meaning is an unknown-but-finite period of time. Every first-year linguist knows the adjective form of a noun can never be stronger than the noun itself. A newspaper delivered to my home once each day is a daily newspaper, not an eternal one. A bill that comes once per month is a monthly bill, not an everlasting bill. However, our translators violated this rule with the adjective forms of age in an effort to keep traditions intact at the expense of common sense and reason. They used terms such as everlasting and eternal instead of age-lasting or seasonal.

I had so much more to say but not enough time, so I finished on a positive note by acknowledging our heavenly Father's care for us—he anticipates the question and promises an answer. When I was done, Terry looked at me and asked, "Does that mean you think everyone will be saved?" I didn't give a direct answer; I danced. I told them it was something each would need to consider for themselves. It was the perfect Texas Two-Step—I kept my promise to the Lord not to be a source of trouble and I put the issue back in the lap of each individual, where it needed to be. However, even though I was less than direct, I believe the Lord caused Terry to ask that question, and in it, a little water was placed on the seeds that were planted that morning.

I don't think any of them were convinced by my words and I often wonder if any of them see it now. Even though my efforts seemed like a failure at the time, the scriptures didn't say in the ages to come Jim Strahan would cause them to see the richness of his kindness; that job has been reserved for the greatest teacher of all.

I will never forget that morning with my friends; all of us learned something. For me, the experience gave me an answer to another question—why hasn't the Lord stepped in sooner to straighten out this mess? Turns out it's a learning process and the Master Teacher will bring us to the right conclusion at the right time. With that answer pocketed, and with an impending move back to San Antonio on the horizon, my family and I left that church fellowship with fond memories, good friends, and no major confrontations over doctrine.

Not long before the move back to Texas, I remember one quiet evening sitting on the front porch of our Nashville home looking up at the stars and asking him what I should do next. I had concluded that the great peace and comfort given to me wasn't going to be spread to others through the traditional church setting. The power of tradition was much stronger than my power to persuade. Was he going to use me in a different way? I felt much like a child who had been given some paper and crayons. I knew my Father wasn't expecting perfection and deep down I knew he would be happy with whatever I drew for him. I also remembered being overwhelmed by the memory of my children's first drawings for me. I could barely make out the images, but I could plainly see the love in them and that had brought tears to my eyes. I was so proud of their time and effort and all I could do was smother them with hugs, kisses and compliments. Would my Heavenly Father feel the same way about me? I began to draw.

Prior to this, I had made several attempts at writing a book about what I had learned, but I didn't feel good about the results. One night I looked on line and ordered two books that had recently been written on the subject; *The Inescapable Love of God* by Thomas Talbott and *What Does The Bible Really Say About Hell?* by Randy Klassen. Wow—were they ever great books! These guys had knowledge and talent . . . they made my previous attempts at writing look fairly pathetic in comparison.

On the porch that evening, I reminded the Lord what I had learned from my experiences in business about the chain of command. I reasoned that if someone wanted to make a change in any organization, it was best to go through the chain of command first. I thought, as a change-maker, I should go to the leaders of the church first. After all, they were much more gifted and talented than me. I reasoned that if I told church leaders my story, they, being led by the Spirit, would quickly realize I was telling the truth. I could also provide them the two great books by Thomas and Randy, to lay out the Biblical and philosophical case. If they caught on, the paradigm shift could begin quickly.

So, I drew up the plan in my mind and presented it to the Lord. I wanted to do something special for him. I quickly enlisted the help of a friend, one who had been highly successful at Thomas Nelson Publishing, and he helped me write my story. I also researched and found the home phone numbers of authors Talbott and Klassen. I did a cold-call to their homes, and both were very understanding as I told them my story and how much I enjoyed their books. I felt so embarrassed because I couldn't get through the conversation without breaking down relating my experience as a child. I had practiced it before the call to avoid choking up, wanting to sound professional, but all of that went to hell, so to speak, and I could not control my emotions. I still can't keep back the tears when I speak about it today. Both men seemed to be very understanding, but I was still mad at myself.

After gaining my composure, I told them of my plan to send my testimony and their books to the pastors of 600 of the largest protestant churches in the country. Of course they were grateful, and I'll never forget the encouragement from Thomas as we finished our conversation about how the Lord might reveal the richness of his kindness in the ages to come. My prayer was this age would come quickly and I thought God was using them with their books. Thomas paused and made this comment, "Wouldn't it be just like him to use the vision of a little boy to lead the way?"

It took a little time to put the plan together and complete the logistics. Fortunately, my friend's work was slow at the time and so I was able to hire him to make it a reality. We tried to make an announcement in the magazine, *Christianity Today*, and I tried to give away some of the two books to a large Christian bookstore in Franklin, Tennessee. But the businessmen in charge at both concerns must not have liked the subject, or thought of me as a fool. I guess they thought it was their job to protect others from guys like me. I found all of this to be strange, but I tried to be understanding. Little did I know it was a sign of things to come. We shipped everything via UPS second day air to make sure it was marked as a special delivery and we waited to hear some good responses.

Well, other than a handful of nice letters and one phone call, most of what we heard was the sound of crickets. The one phone call I received came from a pastor of one of the largest churches in Florida. He had some connections with Franklin, Tennessee and wanted to meet me when he was in town. Our phone conversation was very interesting and respectful. He asked, "You mean I've been wasting all my time trying to get people saved?" I responded that his ministry was fulfilling the great commission, and telling others about Christ was a good thing. We never got the chance to meet as I moved shortly afterward back to Texas.

There was one letter from a famous evangelist whom I sincerely believed was led by the Spirit. He wrote me a personal note and told me he would pray for my ministry. The late Dr. James Kennedy also wrote a letter and said he would keep the two books sent in his personal library for future reference. I appreciated those responses, but that was all we heard.

As a follow-up, we shot a video at my new home in Texas and sent DVDs to the same mailing list. It was what I considered to be a personal touch where they could see me as a really genuine person. In the video, I invited all of them to my home if they were ever in the area and I provided my email address and phone number if they ever wanted to speak to me, or if they had any questions. I did receive a few more responses after the second mailing, maybe a dozen in total, and several of those were requests to take them off my mailing list. We had a few good laughs over those.

Comfortably numb might best describe how I felt when it was over. I was at ease with what I had learned over the years and I had often said that if I were the only person on earth who believed in God's plan to restore and fix all relationships past, present and future, it would not shake my confidence one bit. However, I have to admit, the silence was one of the biggest disappointments in my life. I really thought the leadership of the church would respond to the voice of God in all of this. When that did not happen, I was at a total loss.

I told the Lord I was sorry because the money I spent could have gone to something more useful, like feeding the poor. But I was not giving up on spreading this good news to others who needed to hear it. Since attempts at going through the chain of command were rejected, I would now focus on going directly to the people. I established a website and began posting articles on the subject. Many of them were written by my San Antonio friend, Mike He was a prolific writer and provided some great insight into the Greek language of the scriptures.

We also produced our own radio show called *Let's Talk Bible* that aired 30 minutes each week. We were blessed by the fact that my brother-in-law had a recording studio and we all had a blast making the program each week. Our style was particularly irreverent at times, and I'm sure there were people (like my own parents) who did not appreciate that very much. We played Fleetwood Mac for introductory and closing music, and Homer Simpson was a frequent guest. We challenged the more popular bad news and tried our best to replace it with the good news of the gospel. We told jokes, laughed at ourselves and had a great time for about a year and a half.

We had some very positive feedback and made some new life-long friends. But as usual, there were others who were, uh, less supportive. One listener accused us of "greasing the slide to hell" because we were telling listeners about the extent of God's love for them? I remember responding to the email and respectfully asking a few questions. We never received a response; we knew the person could not answer them. Hopefully, another seed was planted.

But after a while it became too difficult to hold down a full time job, do a radio program and accomplish our next goal . . . writing a book. Organizing and consolidating our thoughts into one readable manuscript was a major challenge for two long-winded guys and it would take another two years to get it done.

6

BREAKTHROUGH

~

The articles posted on our website gave us some practice at writing and would later become the foundation of our book. As before, I had no idea where to start and what contribution Mike and I could make given all of the other great books already written on the subject. However, I was confident the Lord would provide an outline as I felt destined to complete this endeavor. And sure enough, the outline came from a simple question my father asked me one day. Isn't it amazing how the Lord speaks to us in ordinary circumstances when we least expect it? My life is living proof of that . . . sending the coaches, sending the former UPSer, sending me a date, a wife, and now an outline to a book through my father.

My dad's favorite TV minister had produced a sermon entitled, "Is God Fair?" Dad was so intrigued by the message that he bought a tape of it for me and asked if I would listen to it on the hour drive back to my home from his place. Dad lives in Quihi, which is, technically, a "ghost town" near the edge of the west Texas desert midway between Castroville and Hondo. It's hot and dry most of the year, and not much grows out there except cactus, scorpions, rattlesnakes, and silence.

Quihi life is pretty slow and simple. Most of the early German settlers who survived in the area did so by hard work, common sense and a strong desire to be independent, or maybe isolated. My dad has an historical marker on his place that reads, "On this site in 1896, nothing happened." And that proud Quihi tradition continues to this day. Fortunately for our family, that kind of retired atmosphere has allowed mom and dad plenty of time to do what they love most—pray for their loved ones and seek encouragement and strength for them in God's Word. It's also given my dad the opportunity to contemplate perplexing questions like, "Is God Fair?" and hope for his children's sake the answer might be "yes."

I must say from the start that I appreciated the minister's effort to tackle this very tough question. He has a great ministry and anyone who blesses my father and others, has my support. But his answer, "No, God is not fair," made me a bit uncomfortable. So I began searching the scriptures for myself and then discussed the topic with my closest Christian friends. Frankly, we had some very intense moments. I also requested additional input from two other very famous Bible scholars and authors. Thankfully, they both responded in personal letters, but neither of them agreed with the first minister, or with each other. So, I ended up with a full range of definitive answers: No, Yes, and Sometimes.

Well, this was obviously a challenging question. So Mike and I decided to make it part of the title of our book. We also thought the first piece of the puzzle, probably the first chapter of our book, would need to frame the question, establish its importance, and lay out the reasons for all the different answers. So I wrote a draft and circulated it among some close friends. A few said it was too harsh and I needed to tone it down. That really bothered me, because it was not my intention to put anyone down but rather cause them to stop and think for a moment. Maybe my perceived lashing out at the religious establishment was a subconscious result of being rejected by them previously, or maybe it was just my competitive nature; I really didn't know. After hearing this from my friends, I went back over the article but still didn't see the need to change anything. However, if it were a problem, I wanted to fix it. I began to pray in earnest again. I told the Lord I needed his help. My specific prayer was that if my words were poor, then, I needed his words.

Less than a week later, Mike and I were having lunch after church. I had hoped the Lord would send an answer through our minister's sermon or something said in the men's Bible study class that morning. I had listened, but nothing jumped out at me. I was not angry but began to feel a bit frustrated again that God had shown me the best news ever, but apparently, I couldn't convey it without being offensive.

The sticky part of the article was some things I had said about two ministers, James Kennedy and John Hagee. These were highly influential leaders in the church, and they had said some . . . uh, less than accurate things (good choice of words?) and I wanted to take them on. Everybody says some dumb things occasionally, and I think a preacher should be like an athlete evaluating their performance. If a quarterback threw a bad pass, it was okay to admit it and be more determined not to make that mistake again. One of the pastors was a former football player, and I'm sure when he received criticism meant to help the team, he took it like a man and moved on. But realizing I could have been using the wrong approach, I asked the Lord how he would say it.

As we ate, I was telling Mike about my frustration and the need for God's words, not mine. Then a thought popped into my mind. I remembered Mike mentioning a few weeks earlier the "sons of thunder" and asked him to explain the passage in Luke again. He was just getting warmed up, when he suddenly stopped in mid-sentence. I'll never forget the look on his face when he said, "Jim, not even the names have changed!"

Luke 9 featured James and John, and the two pastors I was attempting to refute were named James and John. I had my answer; I didn't need to say anything because Jesus had already said all that was necessary to his two disciples, James and John two thousand years earlier. I went back and replaced my words with the words of Jesus, and posted the finished piece on our first website under the title "Is God Fair?" It's still there in the same form as I wrote it in 2004.

The very first review of the article came from a person named Melanie, a chaplain at a funeral home in Kansas, if my memory serves me correctly. She relayed to me how much she enjoyed the article and was particularly impressed by the kind words directed towards James Kennedy and John Hagee. Seriously! I thanked the Lord for correcting me. I learned that when you don't know what to say, it's always best to let his words do the talking.

In the end, we used the phrase "Sons of Thunder" on the front cover of our book. Later, after it was in the final stages of being published, I learned more about why the passage in Luke was so important to this discussion. Luke's story relays how Jesus, James, and John were passing through Samaria on their way back to Jerusalem. Something was pushing me to go back and look at that story one more time, and below is what I discovered.

The first visit to Samaria was recorded in John 4 where we find Jesus witnessing for two days there with many coming to believe he was the Messiah. There is a lot of symbolism here, the main symbol being that of the Body of Christ ministering in a non-believing world proclaiming the gospel for two days (two thousand years) with many becoming believers. I had a hunch the Luke passage concerned our Lord's second coming to the same area and so I Googled it and checked several sources. Sure enough, this passage was indeed the second record of him being in that area. Before his second coming to this area, here's what we find Jesus doing in the Luke passage—sending out messengers. And notice the language: so that others could prepare for his return. But evidently, there were many who did not believe Jesus was the Messiah, so they rejected him. Sound familiar?

When James and John heard about it, they immediately asked Jesus if he wanted them to call fire down from heaven and consume these non-believers! Obviously, they held the first two views of love's victory and thought it would be in God's will/plan to burn up or annihilate those who refused to accept the Messiah before his second coming. And what was Jesus' reaction to that insanity? He turned and rebuked them. These mistaken ideas were coming from his chosen, some of the ones closest to him!

Sadly, this mindset remains with us to this day, but it is definitely not what Jesus had in mind. After all, he said he did not come to condemn the world, but to save it. Mike and I affectionately call people with this mindset . . . Sons of Thunder (SOT's) because that was the name Jesus gave to James and John.

Nicknames indicate something relevant about a person. One of my best friends growing up was Albert Gonzalez. We called him Speedy because of his quickness on the football field, at least until the end of our freshman year. At that time, he played wingback and we connected on many passes with several of them ending up as touchdowns. During the last game of the season, he caught a pass from me after running a good route, which left him "wide open." I still remember to this day the tension I felt as I threw him the pass. He was so open and it would have been a big embarrassment had I missed him. The pass was only about 30 yards, and fortunately, we connected. However, Speedy was run down from behind before he could score. We still laugh about our coach's comment as he came off the field. It went something like this: "Speedy, next year you're going to be a lineman!" And Speedy became an offensive guard his remaining three years of high school.

When I see James and John on the other side, I plan to nickname them the "Boom Brothers" after the sound of thunder. Their coach nailed them with that SOT moniker when he pulled them to the sideline to bring them up to speed. Thunder is loud and scary when it goes off, but it's nothing more than a bunch of superheated, hot air. I wonder what they will call me in return—maybe STCO (pronounced stucco), meaning, slow to catch on.

The second part of the title to our book was "What About Gandhi?" Before our writing began, Mike and I took some time off and we hiked in the Gila wilderness region of southern New Mexico. I love that area and we wanted to spend a little time discussing the outline of the book and have some fun along the way. I had been reading Lee Strobel's book, *The Case For Faith*, and found the same fairness question couched in a different form and posed to a well-known Christian apologist, Ravi Zacharias. Zacharias speaks to large audiences around the world, and invariably, one of the questions he receives is—what about Gandhi? We know Gandhi never professed faith in Jesus, and the real question resides in the eternal fate of this good man. When Zacharias gets that question, he says, "That's the time I want to take a break." We understand his dilemma because of his entrapment in tradition, and when we read his painful explanation—it's actually not an explanation at all; he just skirts the issue. We say painful because we believe him to be a good man who wants to help others with a satisfying answer but is unable to do so at this point in his training. However, he does do the next best thing when he responds by saying: "Let's leave that to God." That answer is much better than how James and John once responded. (BTW—I love listening to Zacharias, and his book, *Jesus Among Other Gods*, is one of my favorites. He's definitely not a STCO and I think he's very close to seeing love's victory in its entirety.)

So, with the title finished, we were off and writing. From the scriptures, we knew God had stated emphatically that he was fair. And if he is fair, then, we asked two questions in the opening chapter:

Question one: if we know God doesn't show favoritism or partiality, then why did he give Paul an undeniable, hands-on, life changing, miraculous experience and not do the same for others bound for hell or extinction?

Question two: why would an arrogant, sadistic, traitor to his heritage, Pharisee of Pharisees, and proclaimed enemy of Christ get the advantage of ten convincing miracles within three days, and not others, including good people like Gandhi who needed faith as much as Paul?

There were several other spin-off questions in our opening chapter, and when people stuck in Augustine's paradigm are unable to answer them, we noticed they appeal to the "mysterious ways of God" as a way of escape. Mike and I see this as just another step in their training, and we laugh about it now because we can readily recall those moments during our own education when we came to the end of our rope too. God is such a patient teacher and a great coach. When the richness of his kindness finally becomes a reality to all, I can only imagine us laughing together with great joy, especially at our former lives as SOT's, STCO's and whatever other nicknames that could be applied to us all.

Recently, I saw a cartoon which demonstrates the unintended message Christians send to many outside our faith. It was taken from Gary Armirault's Facebook page. Someone sent him a drawing of Jesus knocking on a door and having a conversation with someone on the other side of it:

"It's Jesus; let me in."

"Why?"

"Because I want to save you."

"From what?"

"From what I'm going to do to you if you don't let me in."

Unfortunately, that message sometimes bleeds through the side of our human sorting facility; it's the wrong message, and it's ugly.

With the fairness article done, another good friend asked me what I was going to write about next. His name was also Michael and we had met as first year teachers of math at a local high school. He was an MIT graduate who decided to make a contribution to society by teaching math after a career as a stock broker and tax consultant. With similar motivations and backgrounds in private industry, we connected immediately. I don't recall how the subject of religion came up, but we thought very much alike regarding God's end-game for humanity. Michael had an interesting history as a Messianic Jew. He was one of the most intelligent human beings I have ever met. When I told him of my experiences as a child, he had no problem with it, and we spent many hours discussing that subject along with the inherent problems in our educational system. He is now teaching math at a local college.

When he asked about my next topic, there was no hesitancy on my part—the conversation between Jesus and Nicodemus. I told him and his wife that the exchange in the third chapter of John's gospel had always bothered me and I felt an urge to go look at it again. I had no clue why I was so attracted to it at that point. What had bothered me greatly was a story involving what seemed to be a genuinely troubled man asking some legitimate questions, and Jesus responding with what seemed almost uncaring answers that were too spiritual for anyone to understand. As a teenager, I remember telling the Lord that he didn't need to prove he was smarter than us, and I wished he would have taken it down a few notches for common folks like me. I didn't say it disrespectfully, and I told him we would have to come back to the conversation with Nicodemus later because I didn't get it; it just seemed like one big disconnect. This time, when I began to study the passage, my eyes were opened to what I now consider as one of the most profound dialogues between God and man in the entire Bible. Amazingly, it was a discussion about God's plan to redeem all back to him. I really don't know how I could have missed it all those years.

At the time I was attending a large church in San Antonio. When I finished writing about this subject, the pastor started a series on John 3:16. It lasted several months and I had the opportunity to listen to some very gifted speakers as they relayed the traditional point of view in that passage. The timing was incredible. After a while I began writing the pastor thinking he might find some of my research useful. He responded in an email recognizing that I seemed to have a great amount of knowledge about the passage. I appreciated the compliment but was disappointed that the elephant in the room was being ignored. Later, I wrote to the group of ministers at the church who took turns teaching the subject each Sunday. Little did I know the pastor would publish a book on John 3:16 when the series came to an end. I immediately picked up a copy to see if anything I sent had been included . . . but I walked away disappointed.

The bulk of my correspondence with the leadership of that church was from the article I wrote earlier on the subject. I've included a few exerts from it below because I want you to consider the words of Jesus as he left us a record of how one enters his kingdom. He didn't dance around the issues with subtle persuasion, and his directness put Nicodemus back on his heels.

In order to enter God's kingdom, Jesus said you must be born again by the Spirit. He then compared spiritual birth to physical birth and the action of the Spirit in the process to the action of the wind. He reminded Nicodemus that man does not control the wind. "The wind blows where it wishes, and you hear the sound of it, but cannot tell where it comes from, or where it goes."

The obvious point here (the elephant in the room) is that a child has no more control over its birth than a man has control over the wind. Both physical and spiritual births are a result of an act of love when a father plants a seed (his Word) by his own pleasure. The birth of the child is not dependent on the actions or decisions of the child but on the will of the father. John 1:12–13 states the children of God were born, not "of the will of the flesh, nor of the (free) will of man, but of (the will) God." (KJV) It could not have been stated more clearly.

At that point, Nicodemus nearly went into shock after realizing what Jesus had just said. Since he had been taught all of his life that entry into the kingdom was based upon man's decisions, quite naturally, he responded with, "How can that possibly be?" or, "How can that possibly work with free will?"

Jesus answered by referring him back to a familiar story in the Old Testament regarding Moses lifting up the serpent in the wilderness. "Then the Lord said to Moses, "Make a fiery serpent, and set it on a pole, and it shall be that everyone who is bitten, when he looks at it, shall live." Notice, it is not "everyone who looked" as a subset of all those who were snake-bitten, it was "everyone snake-bitten *when* they see Jesus as the sacrifice for their sins." Again, Isaiah 45:20–24 begins with God calling: "come all ye ends of the earth and be saved," and the calling finishes with every knee bowing and every tongue swearing, "My righteousness and strength is in you."

Jesus said, "If I be lifted up, I will draw all men unto me!" I learned that the Greek word translated "draw" also means to drag in as with a net, sometimes by force. "Then as one man's trespass led to condemnation for all men, so one man's act of righteous leads to acquittal and life for all men," Romans 5:18. These are just a few of the hundreds of scriptures that all carry the same theme, that of God going after every one of the lost sheep until he finds not 99 percent, but 100 percent of them.

How can we miss this? We reason: he can't force himself on us because he desires that his children love him freely. While that is true, we forget, or fail to give him credit for his ability to draw us to him. The argument that a free will agent can resist God forever is unscriptural and illogical. On the contrary, God has written a wonderful plan where "free will" is just another tool in his hand. Thomas Talbott:

> . . . moreover, Pauline theology provides a clear picture of how the end of reconciliation could be foreordained even though each of us is genuinely free to choose which path we shall follow in the present. The picture is this: The more one freely rebels against God in the present, the more miserable and tormented one eventually becomes, the more incentive one has to repent of one's sin and to give up one's rebellious attitudes. But more than that, the consequences of sin are themselves a means of revelation: they reveal the true meaning of separation and enable us to see through the very self-deception that makes evil choices possible in the first

place. We may think we can promote our own interest at the expense of others or that our selfish attitudes are compatible with enduring happiness, but we cannot act upon such an illusion, at least not for a long period of time, without shattering it to pieces. So in that sense, all paths have the same destination, the end of reconciliation, but some are longer and windier than others. . . . As Paul puts it: We are all predestined to be conformed to the image of Christ (see Romans 8:29); that part is a matter of grace, not human will or effort.

God is so smart. He knows when a person finally realizes their miserable, snake-bitten and dying condition, they will cry out for mercy to the One whose mercy endures forever. This moment is precisely "when" God plans to heal them, and why he knows he will dry every tear from every face.

This is the answer to how and when the plan will work. Next, Jesus adds a little extra by telling Nicodemus why he would be lifted up on that cross. From our beginning text, John 3:16, we know he did it out of love to guarantee our ultimate safe entry into his Kingdom and presence. As retired minister, John Gavazonni once wrote:

> It is conventionally presumed that by saying 'whosoever' Jesus was limiting the number of those who would believe in him, who would not perish, and who would have everlasting life. But if one were to look at the Nicodemus conversation in its entirety, they would not find limitation in his words, but underlined and emphasized inclusion of all . . . If I were mayor of a city, knowing that every citizen of that city were certain to claim a local tax refund once it was announced and understood by all, I might assure them up front that whoever applies for the refund will receive it. In that case, 'whosoever' would underline and emphasize that none will be excluded when they come forward. 'Whosoever' gives full force to the fact that the refund is for everyone. The intended effect would be to discourage anyone from thinking that for any reason, they might be disqualified from receiving the refund . . . In the progression of this gospel record, right up front, assurance is given that birth into the Kingdom is a 'given' because of his great love for us. It is God's decision; it is his judgment that: 'there is no name under heaven, given among men, whereby we *must* be saved.'

I believe the essence of this entire late-night conversation is found in heart of Jesus. He did not come to condemn the world, but to set it free. All of us have condemned ourselves by the all-too-apparent sins in our lives, but Jesus paid the price and all that remains is the process whereby we will all be reconciled back to him, and to each other. During this process we should not serve him out of Nicodemus-like fear, thinking we must do everything right, but out of affection because of the free gift of life he secured on our behalf. If he has revealed himself to us now, it's so that we can be an example and a witness of his great love to the rest of the world, and to become a participant in his plan to redeem all in his timing.

The article I wrote about Jesus and Nicodemus eventually became the third chapter in our book. Some of the conversation between them is quite touching. At the beginning of the exchange, Jesus told Nicodemus that he needed to change (that's what rebirth means—to radically change). Brother JV puts it this way, Jesus told the old man, "You need to start over!" Nicodemus responded by asking how, because he was old and stuck in his ways. That sounds familiar. It represents the human condition and how difficult it is to change, especially as we get older. Nicodemus needed to change his mindset, and Jesus was there to help him along the way just as he will be there for everyone else when they call on him.

Within a year after posting the article, I was invited to speak at a church convention in Idaho. I was very hesitant to accept because there were many gifted speakers, notably, one of my mentors, Dr. JV Foster. I felt so inadequate. As it turned out, I was asked to speak twice, and after a great deal of reluctance and much prayer, I decided to do it. I would speak on the topic of God's fairness and the conversation between Nicodemus and Jesus.

I remember telling JV privately how nervous I was and his encouragement before it was my turn to speak. In the first session I taught what I had learned about Jesus and Nicodemus. Afterward, I remember several people asking for my notes and that made me feel like God was at least pleased that I had tried. In the audience was one of the best speakers at the convention, James Bruggeman, who said when I came to the part about no man having control over the wind, the building shook loudly from a strong gust. Others standing around me chimed in that it was kind of eerie, and perfectly timed. I just laughed; who knows?

But the most moving moment came when an elderly man came to the front of the church before I could gather my notes and leave the podium. With tears in his eyes, he shook my hand very hard and could barely get out the words. I could tell he was trying to gather his emotions before he could push it out in a whispered voice: "I've got to start over." He continued to shake my hand and his head yes while attempting to gain his composure.

He had just caught a glimpse of the richness of his kindness for the first time, and it was wonderfully overwhelming. I needed to hear that and it still touches my heart to this day. It was like speaking with Nicodemus.

Some Christian leaders proclaim it is better to withhold this type of information as part of "The Doctrine of Reserve." Their rationale is stated thus: "The mysteries of faith should not be made public without considering the state of the hearers. Teaching must regard the disposition and prior knowledge of the taught, not revealing too much to those not spiritually ready to receive it. There is particular peril in preaching the doctrine of atonement without a concomitant call to repentance and amendment" per Raymond Chapman Professor of English at the University of London and honorary assistant priest at St. Mary's, Barnes. I do think his thoughts have merit. There's a risk that immature believers will take advantage of God's kindness and use their belief in universalism as a license to sin. However, the very heart of this teaching focuses on our motivations . . . we should serve him out of love, not fear. Those who would foolishly take advantage clearly do not understand the nature of sin and its attendant consequences. And if one really wants some heat, try taking advantage of his generosity and end up in the lake of fire . . . not a good idea. On the flip side of the reserve doctrine, there's no excuse to misrepresent out of fear someone can't handle the truth.

With the fairness article done and insight on John 3:16, Mike and I felt we had something new for others to consider surrounding this topic, and we began working in earnest to publish our first book.

7

Holding Faith

~

During the writing of our book, my wife was searching for a smaller and more intimate church environment, so we left that large assembly and found a group of Christians who were meeting at a nearby dance hall. Holding church services there was a very effective use of resources. The beer signs and a picture of a laughing donkey on the wall with the words, *Dance Your Ass Off*, really didn't bother anyone. Once the set-up was done and the music started, that place was rockin! As a matter of fact, it kinda made you wanna . . . dance, sometimes.

We enjoyed the music, people and pastors—two brothers. My wife joined in by helping in the nursery and I volunteered to come in at 5:30 a.m. each Sunday to clean the dance floor and stage before the set-up crew arrived to take care of the chairs and sound equipment. All was going well and I told the Lord I just wanted to enjoy the friendships and stay away from any discussion of my book's topic, because it was obvious this congregation held the traditional view of God's end game.

One Saturday morning, I ran into the lead pastor at Starbucks and we shared a table together. He is a great guy with a huge heart and a good sense of humor . . . another of God's gifted speakers. It was mostly small talk and I really don't remember exactly how the subject came up, but I think we were discussing how we landed in the Boerne area. He was originally from the valley area of south Texas. I told him I had moved here to retire and write a book. He asked about the subject matter and I gave him a quick synopsis. It was a friendly and respectful conversation, although he did not agree with my views. He voiced his concern that it could be very confusing to new Christians and he did not want me to speak about it at church.

There was so much to say at that point, and my competitive nature wanted to take over. I had flashbacks to my days in football and I wanted to line up and take him on. I never tried to hurt anyone while on the field, and I always shook hands with opponents at the end expressing genuine gratitude to be able to compete with them. Life has taught me that if you get a chance to get off the bench and get in the game, you should expect to be knocked down; it's just a part of it. Honestly, I felt it was no different here. As long as we humans are looking through that dark glass mentioned by Paul, we are going to be wrong sometimes. Iron sharpening iron generates heat, but as long as we pick each other up when the play is over, there is no harm and no foul. At least that's my way of looking at it. However, I didn't know if this man wanted to play, and I had previously told the Lord I didn't want to be a source of any controversy. So I gathered myself and told the pastor I would respect his wishes.

Much later, we joined a small group led by the assistant pastor. He and his wife were two of the nicest people I have ever met. He had a great sense of humor too and was musically gifted and administratively strong. His brother had the big vision, but this younger one was the realist who dove into the details to make sure things happened. They obviously complimented each other and it was fun to watch.

After rushing home from work one evening to get my Bible and meet my wife at the small group meeting, the unexpected occurred. As I turned on the alarm system before rushing out the door, a question overwhelmed me: "Tonight, he (the assistant pastor) will ask what your favorite scripture is; what will you say?" I remember stopping in the hallway, pausing, then responding, "Oh no Lord, not again." I just wanted to eat some good food and enjoy the evening with our friends, and I'm sure the Lord didn't mind that either. Knowing my passion and my tendencies, I knew I had to be careful because of the promise I made to his brother. However, I wasn't going to lie about anything either, if asked.

I told the Lord I would give them my two favorites, one from each the Old and New Testament. And when my friend asks me why I chose them, I would try to compose something brief to avoid any potential issues. I told the Lord I appreciated him letting me know in advance so I could be true to him and true to my word. The five minute drive to their home allowed me enough time to put something together.

After a wonderful meal (those people could really cook) we gathered in the den and started our discussion for the evening. I had a big grin on my face because I knew what was coming. After sitting down, he said, "Tonight, I thought we would discuss our favorite scriptures, and Jim, we will start with you. What is your favorite scripture?"

I wanted to laugh because of the joy I felt over the Lord speaking to me previously, but I knew that would have been out of place, so I acted surprised and gave my answer:

Isaiah 45: 22–24 "Look to Me, and be saved, All you ends of the earth! For I am God, and there is no other. I have sworn by Myself; The word has gone out of My mouth in righteousness, And shall not return, That to me every knee shall bow, Every tongue shall take an oath. He shall say, Surely in the Lord I have righteousness and strength."

Romans 5:18 "Then, as one man's trespass led to condemnation for all men, so one man's act of righteous leads to acquittal and life for all men."

He then looked at me with a rather funny look on his face and asked why I chose those two. And I gave a brief answer—because it shows the very heart of God and demonstrates the really good news of the gospel. It felt a little awkward to give such a short answer to what was intended to be an open-ended question, but I held back, and in doing so, I kept my promise. There was a long pause before he moved on to the next person.

Because of the warning, I had dodged a bullet. But how long could this go on? In the back of my mind I wondered if this was a sign of things to come.

At the next small group meeting, he decided to start a great Rick Warren series on "A Purpose Driven Life." At the beginning we read from Ecclesiastes 3:11 using the Revised Standard: "Also he has put eternity into man's mind, yet so that he cannot find out what God has done from the beginning to the end."

The opening question posed to the group was: "What did God mean when he said he has put eternity into man's mind?" I hoped he wouldn't call on me to answer, because short of acting like Sergeant Shultz from Hogan's Heroes . . . "I know nothing" . . . I felt I had to answer honestly.

The entire sentence confused me. None of us can fathom infinity. So, why would God put something in our mind and then tell us he did it so that we cannot find it out? If we can't find out, why bother putting it into our mind? The entire verse seemed like an oxymoron, and very puzzling. Additionally, my radar went up when I heard the word "eternity." Knowing the trouble this word had caused for Bible translators, and having had my curiosity piqued, I knew I would have to do some research in order to offer an intelligent answer. Thankfully, I wasn't called upon that night. The next evening, after looking at the original Hebrew words used in the Ecclesiastes passage, I e-mailed a truthful, but non-confrontational answer to our Small Group leader, the assistant pastor:

TEXT OF MY EMAIL

I had a little fun with that scripture, and here's what I found in Strong's concordance. 'Also he has put . . . ' The word 'also' could have easily been translated 'though.' Choosing which word to use is a matter of choice. As you will see in the following, I believe 'though' is best. Also, there is no punctuation in the Hebrew, so the translators put periods in places they thought best; though I don't think there should be one prior to the word 'also.'

Continuing, 'Though he has put. . .' The word translated 'put' is ok, but other words could have been used as well, like 'caused' or 'assigned,' another choice to make. I think the word 'caused' works best as we shall soon see. Just go with me for now.

'Though he has caused eternity. . .' The Hebrew word, olam, translated 'eternity' is a word that means time that is unknown, veiled or concealed. It does not necessarily mean 'eternity.' As a matter of fact, some translations have used 'world' instead of 'eternity' in this passage. Is it world, or eternity? There is a huge difference!

This word is also found in other phrases like 'the everlasting hills' and once where Jonah described the passage of time when he was in the belly of Shamu, or whomever. Obviously, Jonah did not spend eternity in the fish, but it must have seemed like forever. The time period was concealed, or whaled up, I mean veiled from him while Jonah was causing fish flu. In the darkness, he did not have a little Mickey Mouse watch with phosphorescent hands so that he could tell time with. But later, after the fish called for Ralph when he could not turn Jonah into whale poop, Jonah found out the episode lasted only three days. The hills don't last forever either; but they do last for an unknown period of time. So, could this verse mean that he has caused the timing of the events in our lives to be veiled or concealed?

Take a look at the preceding infamous verses in this chapter. The word 'time' is used 30 times . . . a time for this . . . a time for that . . . a time for the other . . . If Solomon did write this, he must have been a strange man because he forgot your favorite and mine: 'a time to eat!' So, one could easily conclude that 'time' just might have been the main subject on Solomon's mind when writing this chapter.

Continuing: 'though he has caused the time to be concealed in man's mind ...' The word for 'mind' could have been translated 'intellect' or 'understanding.' This same Hebrew word was translated as 'understanding' in 10 other places in the KJV. So, although 'mind' is ok, I prefer intellect or understanding.'

Putting it all together and right after he told us there was a season and time for everything, Solomon concludes with: he has made everything beautiful in its time though he has caused the timing (of these events) to be concealed from man's understanding so that no one can find out the work that God does from beginning to end (the length of time or season).

In other words, no one knows the timing of these events because God has hidden it from our understanding.

Gotta go,

I think it's time to eat, and that's a beautiful thing.

Jim

Applying the true meaning of *olam* as time that is hidden or unknown makes this passage much easier to understand than trying to insert the concept of eternity. It's no wonder that the series started with that question. And the King James translators made it even worse when they translated *olam* as "world" ... Set the world in their heart? What? That square peg just won't go into that round whole.

It's also important to note that the Greek equivalent of *olam* is *aion*. This fact has profound implications. Clearly the translators of the King James, NIV, Living Bible, and the Revised Standard had difficulty rendering both words consistently. If a word can either mean a finite period of time, or an infinite period of time, then, who decides which term should be used—the translator, the tradition of men, the majesterium of the church? When something so controversial is hidden from everyday people, and when those in charge don't want to talk about it, we need to ask ourselves why.

Obviously, somebody goofed in the few Old Testament scriptures discussed above, and with a little time and effort you will soon discover that the translations of these words in many other places are highly suspect, or just flat out wrong. I believe people should be informed about the issues so that they can prayerfully consider them and draw their own conclusions.

In the appendix, I have included a few notes that Mike and I used when covering this topic on our radio program. The English words translators insert in place of *olam* or *aion* have huge implications. I encourage you to educate yourself as much as possible. There is a great article by Alexander Thomson that you may find helpful on the web under the title "Whence Eternity?"

8

Where We Once Stood

~

It has been said, "Don't cry because you are leaving; smile because you were there." And I felt good about our time at that church. These were good-hearted people walking in the light God had given them. However, after the questions at the small group meetings, the email to the assistant pastor, my passion, and the pending book, I felt I could no longer remain silent about my beliefs. After some introspection while on vacation, I wrote a letter of resignation and it was gracefully accepted. We parted ways with a smile, and I do miss the friendships made there.

That vacation was our first trip to Europe. It was fabulous. We visited parts of France, Germany, Austria and Switzerland, and all of them were so beautiful and rich in history. I agree with travel specialist Rick Steves when he said, "If Heaven isn't what it's cracked up to be, send me back to Gimmelwald, (Switzerland)."

One of the most interesting days was spent visiting the Dachau Concentration Camp Memorial site. At first, I really didn't want to go as I figured I knew what it was all about and I wanted to spend more time visiting the local beer gardens around Munich. It was a darn near perfect day with cool temperatures and blue skies, and I wanted to be outside. However, my wife, daughter and son-in-law spent almost the entire day inside the museum reading every word on every picture and historic display, totally mesmerized by the descriptions of the conditions inside the former camp.

I moved through the displays a bit quicker and had some time alone thinking about their historical significance. Here was a place where people were imprisoned, tortured, annihilated and burned for being different, either politically, religiously, or even physically. They were considered dangerous and had to be removed from society. It wasn't just about being Jewish; it was anyone who did not share the same set of beliefs as those in power.

What caught my eye in some of those pictures from the past were the buildings surrounding the area. I had always thought this camp was in some isolated place where these activities could be hidden. However, for at least thirteen years, the atrocities were committed right where people like you and me lived, and not much was done about it. One has to wonder what common folks were thinking. With so many people working in and around this very large facility, over such a long stretch of time, the ugliness could not have gone unnoticed.

Were common people just afraid to say anything? I think that might have been the case. And what led to the justification of these horrors in the minds of those who thought they were in the right? Many books have been written trying to determine how this tragedy could possibly have happened. I think history will agree that the insanity seemed to have its roots grounded in a national sense of fear, anger and despair after years of devastating war and oppression that comes with defeat. And when the misguided filled the void, cruelty, chaos and conformity followed—a sad statement about the human condition. As I sat outside on one of the benches of the compound on that very beautiful day, I thought about how lucky I was to be alive and how difficult it was for those who suffered, for those who were misled, and for those who fought on both sides.

And then another question began to trouble me—what would I have done had I been there? It was easy to imagine myself as a liberator fighting for the oppressed, but what if I had been a German? As a common everyday person just trying to make it through life, how would I have reacted to the situation? Would I have had the courage to stand up and say or do something positive? We will never know, but the thought of me riding the status quo was both humbling and sad.

As I considered my own weakness and intolerance of others who do not look or think the way I do, I began to notice some ominous parallels. For centuries Christians, including those closest to Jesus, have believed it justifiable to imprison, torture, annihilate and burn others eternally, just because they hold a different set of beliefs. No, I don't know any Christians who would do such things now, but they don't have any problem with their god doing it! I believe the idea of God damning people eternally to be an appalling misrepresentation of his character and plan for mankind, and I believe its embrace has been a stumbling block for many throughout the history of the church.

In the past, some have actually acted upon these beliefs and the results were horrible. Queen Mary I, daughter of King Henry VIII and his first wife burned to death over 280 "heretics" who were not Roman Catholic. She expressed her views on the matter as follows: "As the souls of heretics are to be hereafter eternally burning in hell, there can be nothing more proper than for me to imitate the divine vengeance by burning them on earth." For her part, history has tagged her as Bloody Mary and I can hardly disagree with that label.

It's already difficult enough for people to find God given the fear, anger, despair, oppression, unfairness and injustice in this present evil age, and Christians don't need to pile on by misdirecting others with false images of God. Faith is a gift given in his timing and if my eyes have been opened, the light was revealed so that I could point others to a loving Heavenly Father. He has great plans for us; he is not some monster ready to damn people forever if they can't see things the way Christians do during their very short time on earth.

Think about it for a moment; what would have happened to you and me had we been raised as a Muslim or a Hindu? What makes us any better than them? I submit nothing, for they are equally loved by God. Everything I have learned in life to this point tells me that if we by unmerited favor have been blessed with the gift of faith, then our duty is to participate in his plan as he brings others to it in his timing.

I'm not saying those Christians who don't believe the way I do are Nazis. That would be hypocritical and crass. To do that I'd have to put James and John, the ones Jesus chose, in that same category. That is simply not the case. I'm just relaying my development as openly as I can, and I want you to see the sources of my motivation. So, in the remaining hours of that very enlightening day, I came to the conclusion that I needed to stand up and say something. I merely want Christians to consider the obstacles we may be placing in front of others. I've often wondered how the rest of the world views us.

I also ask Christians to consider the attitude of Moses. In Exodus we find God telling him that his anger was burning hot against the children of Israel because they had made a golden calf for worship. He said he was going to consume them with fire because of their sin. As for Moses, God would start over and make him and his family a great people and take them to the Promised Land instead. What an honor! However, Moses stood in the gap for these sinners by telling God, and I'm paraphrasing, "If you don't take them, I will not go. If you do that, what will the unbelieving world (Egyptians) say about you?" Later, Moses prayed that if God would not forgive these sinners, then, he asked God to "blot me out of Your book that You have written." I've never heard anyone pray that kind of prayer! Shortly afterwards, Moses was called God's friend.

This wasn't a case of Moses changing God's mind either; this was relayed to us to increase our understanding of God's heart. When Moses was willing to sacrifice everything—his very life—for the salvation of others, he wanted exactly what God wanted—even if Moses didn't know it at the time. Once Moses pleaded for mercy on behalf of those who had rejected him, his heart matched God's heart, and that is why they became friends.

This is a beautiful picture of who God is, but we contend few see it. Later, Moses asked God to show him his ways that he might "know him" and verify "his grace." Our Father's response was to let Moses see "his goodness." And when God gave a fleeting glance of just the backside of God's goodness, his countenance was immediately and visibly changed for "the skin of Moses' face shone." This, I contend, is the brightness around him. It is his goodness; it is his grace. This is the essence of God.

I wrestled with including the story of my experience at Dachau, fearing others would find it too offensive and draw analogies where none were meant. But this is part of my story, and so I decided to include it as part of the record. The trip was a very thought-provoking experience that I'll never forget, and I offer it as food for thought and discussion.

I'll finish this chapter with a brief summary of a conversation between Mike and me over dinner the other day. He told me he woke up unusually early at 4:00 a.m. a few days prior with something on his mind that Jesus had said to his disciples. Christ once warned them to "Beware the leaven of the Pharisees." Some say leaven was symbolic of sin. That may be true, but why in this case did Jesus single out the leaven of the Pharisees? He could have used the sin of anyone. To make a long story short, it turns out this leaven was what the Pharisee's taught—entrance into God's Kingdom would be based on a man's ability to fulfill the Law—man's own righteousness, man's own choices (the mindset of Nicodemus).

Independence and self-reliance are good things. As leaven makes bread rise, these traits also make a woman or a man rise to the top in everyday life. However, they won't be enough for our salvation. Our efforts, our righteousness, will fall short. But the good news—he will gladly give us his righteousness on our behalf.

But Mike saw something else. He asked if I'd ever wondered why God told the Israelites to get rid of their leaven seven days prior to their exit from Egypt at the time of Passover? If leaven was merely symbolic of sin, why wouldn't he tell them to get rid of it period? So what is the real reason they weren't allowed to use yeast during this time?

Yeast is a good thing; it makes bread easier to eat than bread made without it. And bread made with yeast looks more inviting too. Mike posits that in the arena of salvation, self-reliance, our yeast which puffs up a man, won't be able to bring us out of Egypt (the world) and take us to the Promised Land.

Jesus was crucified at Passover, and he is the only One who can and will provide what we need to get us there. The only way to the Father's Kingdom is through the Son. Jesus is the Way; the only way.

My whole life's story, including that incredible vison at age seven, and everything in the many decades since is neatly summarized by Paul in Ephesians 2:4-7: "But God who is rich in mercy, because of his great love with which he loved us, even when we were dead (asleep) in trespasses, made us alive (woke us up) together with Christ, and raised us up together (takes us off the floors of this life), and made us sit together (indicating a life of companionship) in heavenly places (places of peace and comfort) in Christ Jesus, that in the ages to come (as we mature) He might show the exceeding richness of his kindness toward us in Christ Jesus."

There is no room for leaven, self-righteousness, in salvation's equation. Will good people make it to heaven? Sure. But they won't be there because of their goodness; they will be there because of his. When Christians get all tied up in knots trying to explain a rather monstrous-looking god who destroys or tortures non-believers like Gandhi, the tendency is to go back to the Old Covenant, the Covenant of the Law. "Uh, well, uh...I think good people (by their own works) are going to make to heaven." This is the trap Ravi Zacharias recognizes, and avoids by silence.

In Galatians and in so many other places Paul states the purpose of the Law was to bring us the knowledge of sin and prove that without his essence (love) living in our hearts, we are unable to keep it! It's like a mirror that shows us who we really are when we are not motivated by a heart of love. The Law Covenant produces death, and we need Jesus to stand between us and it as he is the only way to life.

The perfect demonstration of this is found in the Old Testament story where the people of Beth-shemesh made the fatal mistake of removing the Ark's cover (called appropriately the *kappereth* or mercy seat) and 50,000 people fell over dead! The laws of God were kept inside the Ark, and death is what occurs when there is nothing standing between us and the law. Their deaths were meant to teach humanity that "the letter of the law killeth." Thank God Jesus nailed the Law to the cross on our behalf!" That which can only kill, he put to death.

So when someone starts going down that path—"I think good people might make it to heaven," I want to immediately throw down the red flag—beware the leaven of the Pharisees! Let's not go back to where we once stood; let's move forward in grace and grow in the knowledge of what he has already provided.

It pains me to see poor messaging of the Gospel becoming a hurdle to those who want to find God. But there's another even bigger difficulty for those trying to find him—the unfairness of life. One example is the Beth-shemeth incident and what appears to be God's hands-off approach at times. This topic was the subject of what seemed like a thousand conversations between Mike and me over meals, coffee, or my favorite food group—dessert. Before doing the radio program, or writing our book, we met nearly every week to discuss this subject at length. Mike had struggled with it mightily as I had, and after a few years I suggested he reduce it to writing. The next chapter is most important—it's a vital missing piece of the puzzle.

9

BEYOND THIS MOMENT

~

WITH A LITTLE HELP FROM MY FRIEND, MIKE MEEKER

If the kiss of life comes from the things we learn through experience, then what we learn from the experience of others is life's warm embrace. I consider those who have impacted my life as such to be gifts from heaven. In the case of Mike I believe God sent him my way if for no other reason than to help me with this last difficult issue. The answers were sitting in front of me all along right there in his Word, but I needed a friend to help me sort them out; I needed a friend who would listen and not condemn my blindness and subsequent bewilderment.

Mike also needed a friend, and I believe I was sent to listen and offer encouragement as he worked through the final stages of releasing his pent-up anger. As we will see in the pages that follow, he had been wounded in his youth by the unfairness of life and had become a victim of the same poor messaging of the Gospel that we have been talking about to this point in the book. As a result, all he could see was some bad-ass god with a love-me-or-else attitude, and the threat of eternal damnation or annihilation to him was like the Sword of Damocles hanging over our collective heads. In his own words: "At that point, I was damaged goods."

Our genuine desire to lift each other up, and our push for more understanding, worked for both of us. Over time, our discussions led to this chapter and a clear picture in our minds of why evil exists and persists for now. Ultimately, it led to trust without borders in our Heavenly Father as the following pages demonstrate.

This mountain-top view with all its freedom would not have been possible had we not embraced our deep-seated ambivalence. The steep climb out of the valley of frustration was full of raw but honest conversations where word choices were not always charming. However, looking back, I'm glad I had a friend who favored candor over religious pretense. After all, our Creator can see right through us, and there is no value in pretending. Jesus, the man, didn't pretend when he cried out, "Father, why have you forsaken me?," and neither should we.

It would have been all too easy to end the book now, having shown the reality of a Savior with a personal demonstration of his love and care for me. However, I felt the need to address the cruel realities of this present age and the seemingly contradictory idea of a loving Creator who allows injustice, evil, pain and sorrow to flourish lest I open myself to the charge of wearing rose-colored glasses and being hopelessly out of touch. The challenge to the good news expressed in my story is most easily contrasted with one of the most common and anguished questions a human being can ask: "How can you believe in a God that loves me when _____?" Just fill in the blank with whatever tragedy or list of tragedies that have befallen you during your time on Earth that God either failed to protect you from, or worse, outright brought upon you.

I can hear it now, "Well, that's his story. Jim may have lived a charmed existence, but even a cursory look at history shows that millions of others never had such experiences, nor ever will. Just because you've lived a charmed life, doesn't mean most have had it as easy. It may well be that only a few are destined to ever enjoy the same level of blessing you have enjoyed. What about the millions—indeed, billions—who are doomed to never experience the events and blessings you have had?"

The material in this chapter is how I answer that and other difficult questions related to it. I enlisted my friend's help in writing it and have taken excerpts from Mike's unpublished chapter, one left out of the pages of our first book. It would have been entitled: *It's Okay to Trust in God—Just Don't Expect Too Much*. It was written to answer why God does not openly intervene in every human affair. The bulk of this chapter's contents are his.

For now though, I want to give you a brief overview of our position and the evidence that has led us to it. Specifically, Mike

- Discusses several personal tragedies that he suffered in the loss of his parents
- Discusses several disasters—those generated by man—such as the scourge of war

- Discusses several disasters—those labeled as acts of Nature or of God
- Discusses biblical guidance concerning such events whether "acts of God" or man-made.

He shows that all these events draw the same inescapable and grim conclusion that God limits his intervention into the events of this age because *He must!* If he intervened, if it ever became widely known that he really does exist,

1. Human behavior would change drastically, but not for the right reasons, thus circumventing the very purposes he wants to achieve in order to prepare every member of mankind for sharing eternity with him and each other.
2. The possibility of learning many of life's most important lessons would be rendered impossible.
3. His efforts to reflexively generate the desire for the eventual destruction of evil within each individual, replacing it by an even more intense and overpowering hunger for goodness and righteousness would be thwarted.
4. God would be prevented from achieving his ultimate goal of making mankind into the image of his Son, Jesus.

This discussion, I am afraid, is necessary because too many believers—way too many believers—have been given an unrealistic portrayal of what God will do for them in times of crisis only to be devastated when those times arrive and God seems nowhere to be found. Some believers have become disillusioned when they conclude that they or their loved ones have been "betrayed" by God; when the promises, as they understood them, failed to materialize. I am afraid that I myself have been remiss in teaching a proper understanding of God and his promises, and those I love most dearly have suffered because they were not prepared for times when God said "no" and the inevitable disappointments that came in the wake of their frustrations and blindness.

In spite of all of this, to be sure, there is still great news for the believer, genuine comfort to be gleaned from the promises of God and leaned on during the many troubles of this age. God has already given so many gifts to those who trust him: his righteousness, sanctification, redemption, salvation, and a new body. The receipt of these gifts, these treasures in heaven, await our arrival on the other side. But until the time that all of these gifts are realized, the harsh realities of life as described in this chapter *will not relent*. It is part of our development, just as the treasures above are part of our destiny beyond this moment.

To this point in the book, I have written about all the wonderful times God has intervened in my life so openly that it was impossible to miss his care. However, I have not been immune to suffering, nor can any of us expect to be. Barring his second coming, you and I will experience many more disappointments, up to and including death. While this chapter may not be able to ease whatever situation you find yourself in, it may help you understand why God seems so far away when you find yourself in such times of trouble and woe. With that introduction, below is a much needed reality check from Mike Meeker:

IT'S OKAY TO TRUST IN GOD—JUST DON'T EXPECT TOO MUCH

We're going to look at some really horrific events, both personal and historical. In the cold light of objectivity we are going to ask why God didn't do anything in the following events. After reflecting on the advice of Godly counsel—thanks for the insight Paul—I decided to arrange the contents of this chapter differently than originally laid out. My training in humility suggested the best place for my own experiences was to put them last. However, it was pointed out to me that people connect personally and intimately most deeply during the tragedies of life. And that's because we all have suffered losses. That being the case, I hope the reader will forgive me if I take the liberty of talking about myself first and then the selected historical events, second. Not surprisingly, the losses in my own life have impacted me to my core and the lessons I learned from them have caused me to reflect soberly and honestly. I can tell you my disappointment in the God who supposedly "cares so deeply about me"—as I was told repeatedly throughout the years by any number of well-meaning preachers and teachers—was exceeded only by the rage I directed at him—the One who claimed to be My Shepherd. My experiences resulted in me forming the sad view that the words and promises of the twenty-third Psalm were just words on a page. Actual experience has shown me that The Lord is anything but a shepherd. In fact, my walk mirrors far more closely the words of Ecclesiastes 2:22–23:

> For what hath man of all his labour, and of the vexation of his heart, wherein he hath laboured under the sun? For all his days are *sorrows*, and his *travail* grief; yea, his heart taketh not rest in the night. *This is also vanity*. (KJV, emphasis mine)

When I needed him most during the losses in my life, he always seemed to be conveniently out of town. Truth is, I don't know where the hell he was—all I know is that he wasn't anywhere around me. Hell, he may have been the One who caused all my disasters—after all, he is sovereign over all things, right?

Anyone who has reached a certain age will likely be impacted by tragedy of one form or another. Proverbs 14:10 "Each heart knows its own bitterness, and no one else can share its joy." (NIV) I am sure the reader is well aware that usually it is just a matter of time before we have to say goodbye to someone we love or to someone who loves us. There are millions of such *personal* events that occur every year that never reach the pages of the local newspaper or the six o'clock news. So much tragedy is endured privately, intimately and personally. Likely the reader can reflect on at least one but probably more such losses in his/her life at this point.

THE ROLE OF PERSONAL EVENTS—THE DEATH OF MY DAD AND THE LOSS OF MY MOTHER

My dad died on July 15, 1973 at the age of 59. You can guess that I think he died too soon. I had a great dad. (It wasn't until I had reached my early twenties that I was shocked to learn that some of my fellow classmates and other kids grew up in a world where they were actually afraid of their fathers. It just never occurred to me that some fathers were monsters. How naïve I was—but having a great father, it was very easy to assume that all kids had great fathers.) Words fail me to be able to describe how special he was to me. He and his wife graciously reached out and adopted my brother and me into their family and gave me their name. I was 15 when he died of an aggressive cancer over an eighteen month period. It was a horrible death. His departure robbed me of several years of guidance that I could ill-afford to lose.

The day he died our main and associate preachers—Stan and Jerry—came to visit and comfort us. They failed miserably in this endeavor, at least as far as I was concerned. The senior pastor succeeded in uttering a totally thoughtless and useless comparison between my dad's death and the death of Christ. "Just remember Mike, my Lord died at age thirty-three." While he was technically correct, his point was irrelevant. Enraged, I met his eyes, nodded, glanced at Jerry and then looked away. It meant nothing to me that Jesus died at age thirty-three. "So what?" I asked myself, still fuming. Jesus wasn't lying dead in a bed fifteen feet from me—an emaciated shell of his former self, looking more like an Auschwitz victim than a human being. My dad was. Jesus died to save the world, but at that moment I couldn't have cared less what Jesus had done or what he had suffered—after all he wasn't there that morning when my dad died, nor had he done squat to stop it.

My mother remained unmarried for the rest of her life. Too many times I went to sleep hearing her sobbing over the loss of the finest man she ever knew. "He was irreplaceable," was her response to me when I asked if she ever would consider marriage again. And after serving the Lord for more than seventy years, he saw fit to let her mentally deteriorate into oblivion. She didn't recognize me during her last four years—neither did she recognize her natural children, nor even her own name. After suffering through breast cancer and a heart attack, my mother lived out the remainder of her days in a twilight zone existence where all she ever knew that was good had been taken from her. (God—if he was a loving God—should have taken her to her rest long before then, in my estimation.)

My losses are hardly unique. But as I was powerless to stop any of them, so also was God. Why? He is all-powerful—or so my fellow believers assure me. And my own losses are nothing compared to the historical losses the family of man has experienced over the passage of time, whether because of the evil of men, or the evils of nature, or even those of God himself. (Way too many of my fellow believers balk at the idea that God ever does evil, but the Bible has no problem admitting that he does: 2 Chr 34:24 reads, "Thus saith the LORD, Behold, I will bring *evil* upon this place, and upon the inhabitants thereof, even all the curses that are written in the book which they have read before the king of Judah." (KJV, emphasis mine) The editors of the NIV were apparently too uncomfortable with this rendering and its obvious implications to let it stand, so they rendered this verse as: 2 Chr 34:24 "This is what the LORD says: I am going to bring disaster on this place and its people—all the curses written in the book that has been read in the presence of the king of Judah." (NIV) And the silly explanations I've heard or read over the years for the clear rendering of Isaiah 45:7 which reads, "I form the light, and create darkness: I make peace, and create evil: I the LORD do all these things" (KJV) run the gamut of improbable to ridiculous. For my part, I have no trouble believing God does evil without being evil. To me it's a bit embarrassing that this is even an issue—it ought to have settled this issue once and for all a long time ago. By the way, the word rendered *evil* in Isaiah 45:7 (#07451, Strong's Concordance) is the same word rendered evil in 2 Ch 34:24 and in many other verses like 2 Chr 22:4 "Wherefore he did evil in the sight of the Lord like the house of Ahab: for they were his counsellors after the death of his father to his destruction." (KJV)

Historical losses, whether natural or man-made—are like my personal losses except far broader in scope and effect and in the sheer number of people who were affected by them. And so far as I can tell, what I said above is true about historical events in general and these events in particular: God limits His intervention into the events of this age because *he must!* Some of these events below took place over several days, others in a matter of hours. Some happened in conflicts lasting several years. No doubt all of them had lasting impact on the people who remained. Broadly, we want to examine events where man is clearly the culprit for the outcome of the events—or where nature is clearly the culprit—and then consider the role of individual or personal events in our understanding of God and his ways.

THE ROLE OF MANKIND—PEARL HARBOR

America entered World War II after Japan carried out a successful attack on the U.S. Navy stationed at Pearl Harbor on December 7, 1941. That morning there were eight capital targets in the harbor, battleships of the line: *The U.S.S. Arizona*, *The U.S.S. California*, *The U.S.S. Maryland*, *The U.S.S. Nevada*, *The U.S.S. Oklahoma*, *The U.S.S. Pennsylvania*, *The U.S.S. Tennessee*, and *U.S.S. West Virginia*. In a very brief two-hour period, the Japanese inflicted varying degrees of destruction on these proud ships, the ships anchored along Battleship Row.

Historians tell us that 2,403 soldiers, sailors and Marines lost their lives that morning. Out of these eight ships, however, one ship—the *Arizona*—seems to have been singled out for utter destruction. In fact, almost half of the people killed that morning—1,177 sailors—died in a frightful moment around 8:05 a.m. A B5N2 "Kate" high-level bomber dropped a converted 1,500-kilogram armor-piercing shell from an altitude of around 10,000 feet. The bomb punctured the *Arizona's* deck just behind the number two turret, punched through four or five decks and exploded in the ship's forward magazine. Over a million pounds of TNT and high explosives detonated, incinerated 1,177 of the *Arizona's* crew and crumpled the battleship's forward structure like it was tin foil. A wall of fire engulfed the forward half of the battleship and burned for hours. Body parts rained down all around the crippled ship.

The battleship moored just ahead and on the outside of the *Arizona* was the *West Virginia*. Kate torpedo bombers from *Akagi*, *Kaga*, *Hiryu* and *Soryu* skimmed low over the surface of Pearl Harbor and dropped their torpedoes, aimed at the bowels of the unprotected outside battleships. In a very short period of time *Oklahoma*, *West Virginia* and *California* all were reeling from punctured hulls. Both the *Oklahoma* and *West Virginia* took at least seven torpedoes apiece. The *Oklahoma* took on water so fast, that she literally rolled over 180 degrees, her superstructure resting in the harbor mud. Only swift counter flooding saved the *West Virginia* from a similar fate. *West Virginia*, on fire, surrounded by a pool of her own burning oil slowly settled to the bottom of Pearl Harbor.

The Japanese air armada, having strewn Death far and wide, returned to their six carriers leaving Pearl Harbor shattered and many ships of the U.S. Navy wrecked and on fire. The era of the battleship died that morning too and was replaced by the ascendancy of the aircraft carrier. The attack that morning forever settled the question whether battleships were obsolete. For their part, the Japanese had lost twenty-nine aircraft and fifty-five airmen—losses which the Japanese deemed "acceptable," considering the magnitude of the risk they had undertaken and the loss they could have suffered had things not gone well for them.

In a few days the fires were put out, and the dead buried. Well, at least most of the dead. To the horror of the cleaning crews, they began to hear metallic tapping sounds coming from inside the bruised hulls of the *West Virginia* and *Oklahoma*. The tapping heard on *West Virginia* came from desperate men trapped well below the waterline. Sentries posted to guard the wounded ships could hardly bear to stand their posts because they could do nothing for those doomed below. Thankfully, salvage crews were able to cut a hole in the *Oklahoma* freeing some of those trapped inside her. These men emerged the next day feeling as they had walked out of a literal grave. The men in the *West Virginia* weren't so lucky.

From the website, http://www.bartcop.com/0658.htm, we learn the brief history of the *West Virginia* following the attack on December 7, 1941. The bold statement is what we wish to discuss now. In an almost clinical fashion, we learn the collective fate of seventy of her crew:

"*West Virginia* was refloated on May 17, 1942 and moved to Drydock Number One on June 9. Upon further inspection, it was found that seven torpedoes had exploded in her hull. Seventy bodies were also discovered and it was determined that some of these men survived until December 23. After temporary repairs were made, she was moved to Puget Sound for modernization. In September 1944, she returned to the fleet and participated in several actions. She was decommissioned January 9, 1947 and sold for scrap August 24, 1959 to Union Minerals and Alloys Corp., New York."

The Brightness around Him

The website http://www.usswestvirginia.org/uss_west_virginia_history.htm, gives us at least one explanation of how the December 23 date was determined:

> During the ensuing repairs, workers located seventy bodies of *West Virginia* sailors who had been trapped below when the ship sank. In one compartment, a calendar was found, the last scratch-off date being December 23. The task confronting the nucleus crew and shipyard workers was a monumental one, so great was the damage on the battleship's port side. Ultimately, however, *West Virginia* departed Pearl Harbor for the west coast and a complete rebuilding at the Puget Sound Navy Yard at Bremerton, Wash.

There was at least one other way the December 23 date was known; that was also the day when the tapping stopped.

There are some questions worth considering:

What did God find so objectionable about the men on the *Arizona* that he would allow the slaughter of so many of them? After all, there were eight battleships in the harbor that morning, nine if you count the obsolete target battleship *Utah*. The *Pennsylvania*, *Maryland* and *Tennessee* barely got scratched compared to the damage the Arizona suffered. Death was meted out at best randomly, at worst capriciously.

Why did he sentence the men on the *West Virginia* to such a horrific death? You may say, "God, didn't do these things to those men, the Japanese did." Fair enough. But then why didn't God do anything to save the lives of the men that he could have helped? After all, three of those men were still very much alive long after the Japanese had departed the scene. At least the lives of men on the *Arizona* were snuffed out quickly, presumably feeling no pain as they made their transition from this life. The twenty-something-year-olds on the *West Virginia*, in contrast, continued to wait for a rescue that never came. So just where was God on December 7, 1941?

Many believers prattle on about God's providential care, but the reality is that when you take a cold, hard look at the data, it is easy to conclude that his providential care is all but worthless.

The next three stories reinforce this uncomfortable conclusion but the supply of stories that illustrate his apathy, ineffectiveness or outright hostility to the human condition *that he caused* is practically endless. I have shortened them from their original length which basically means I am just going to relate the grim details as history recorded them. Even today, these events have a profound effect on me. Although I am providing shortened versions, I would highly recommend the reader take the time to review each event more fully.

The stories are: 1) The Sacrificial Lambs of VT-3, VT-6, and VT-8—June 4, 1942; 2) The Slaughter at Stalingrad; and 3) The Bloodiest Day in U.S. Military History.

THE SACRIFICIAL LAMBS OF VT-3, VT-6, AND VT-8

Most Americans have never heard of VT-3, VT-6, and VT-8. These designators were assigned to three carrier air groups called Torpedo 3, Torpedo 6, and Torpedo 8, respectively during World War II, in the Pacific theater. The fifteen TBD-1 "Devastator" torpedo bombers of Torpedo 8 (VT-8) were assigned to the *U.S.S. Hornet*, while the fourteen planes of Torpedo 6 (VT-6) were assigned to the *Enterprise*, and the twelve planes of Torpedo 3 (VT-3) were assigned to the Yorktown.

The *Hornet, Enterprise,* and the *Yorktown* were the last offensive weapons the U.S. had in the Pacific theater after the crippling attack on Pearl Harbor. This force steamed toward the Midway Islands atoll located deep in the Pacific Ocean in early June 1942 hoping to ambush the Japanese. (The role of the broken Japanese Naval Code, JN25 played in gaining victory for America is fascinating.)

These forty-one aircraft lumbered into the sky early on June 4, 1942 to destroy the unaware Japanese fleet, consisting of four large aircraft carriers and escort ships. (Their targets were the *Akagi, Kaga, Hiryu* and *Soryu*—four of the very same ships that had launched the crushing attack on Pearl Harbor just six months earlier.)

By the end of the day, only six of these planes returned to their carriers. For those of you who are inclined to do the math, that's an 85 percent loss of life and planes. The nature of battle in June 1942, as these men experienced it, was such that when they left their carriers, they knew they were likely flying one-way missions. As the ordnance they were trying to deliver was a torpedo, successful delivery necessitated that the pilots had to fly in controlled, straight lines as they made their approaches to their targets. This requirement made it particularly easy for the much-faster Zeros to pounce and easily shoot them down—one by one, each spiraling into the vast blue ocean. In spite of the heroic sendoff Lt. Commander John Waldron, the leader of VT-8, gave to his fellow warriors, "If there is only one plane left to make a final run-in, I want that man to go in and get a hit. May God be with us all. Good luck, happy landings, and give 'em hell," they learned the hard way that God may have only been with a few. The bravery of these men—and millions more like them—is hard to fathom. In retrospect, Waldron's wish that "God be with us all" seems now to be, at best, poignantly naïve, or worst, completely moronic.

You might have hoped that having to fly at a certain height and speed—and therefore making yourself a sitting duck for those who wanted to kill you—was restricted only to the torpedo bombers of our previous story. Sadly, this wasn't true. Lacking fighter cover, these bombers had to reach an IP—an Initial Point selected for that mission—and then fly straight to the target du jour, maintain a fixed altitude and path to the target and then drop their bombs in synchronicity with the lead plane's bombardier. When it dropped its load, the rest of the bombers followed suit. Not surprisingly, the results of these missions were often horrific for the bombers and crews of the B-17s and B-24s as they made their steady and naked approaches to the target meeting the full wrath of the German Luftwaffe and AAA head-on. (Of the 12,732 B-17s produced between 1935 and May 1945, 4,735 were lost in combat.)

STALINGRAD

Realizing all hope was lost, Friedrich von Paulus, in command of what remained of the 6th Army, started forming plans for surrender. Realizing this, and hoping to rescue something of the battle, Hitler promoted him to Field Marshal on January 30, 1943. No German Field-Marshal had ever been taken alive in war, and it was hoped this would force him to fight on, or take his own life.

Instead, von Paulus saw this as yet another example of Hitler's increasing irrationality. On January 31, 1943 von Paulus ordered the 6th Army to surrender on February 2. A force of 300,000 was now reduced to only 91,000 tired and starved men. The Soviets force-marched them to detention camps, many dying of starvation on the way. Only some 5,000 would return to Germany after the end of the war.

By any measure the battle of Stalingrad was one of the bloodiest battles in modern history, with some 300,000 Germans killed or captured. Soviet battle deaths were at least 400,000, possibly much higher, with more than 100,000 civilians killed in Stalingrad and its suburbs. No accurate figures have been given for the numbers of Italian and Romanian soldiers killed in the battle.

Wikipedia summarizes the losses as follows: "In all, the battle resulted in an estimated total of 1.7–2 million Axis and Soviet casualties." These figures of soldiers and civilians killed are from just this one six-month battle during WWII. America suffered the loss of around 225,000 soldiers from 1941 through 1945. Why all this carnage? Apparently, these people all died for the sake of two—count 'em, two—maniacal, power-mad men, Adolf Hitler and Josef Stalin.

When World War II concluded, the grim task of counting the dead started. One estimate that I've seen over the years is that World War II consumed the lives of about 50 million people—about equally split between combatants and civilians. We may be able to explain the deaths of so many people because we know that Hitler, Stalin, Bolshevism, communism and National Socialism were all evil entities. There is no reason for us to be surprised that evil consumes the lives of people. But how can we begin to explain such seeming indifference on the part of God—a being that professes love of all his creatures—for not stepping in to stop this carnage before it started?

THE WAR BETWEEN THE STATES—ANTIETAM

There is a creek that snakes its way just west of Sharpsburg Maryland. Its name is Antietam. History being what it is, those living outside this sleepy little town or its creek might never have heard of either were it not for a horrific battle that occurred there in 1862. One contemporaneous account of the battle is still a poignant reflection on man's seemingly limitless ability and willingness to kill other men. http://www.eyewitnesstohistory.com/antiet.htm:

> The two armies met in the Maryland farm fields bordering the trickling Antietam Creek near the town of Sharpsburg. The Union named the conflict the Battle of Antietam in honor of the creek while the South called it the Battle of Sharpsburg in honor of the town. From dawn till dark on the 17th the two armies threw frontal attacks at each other, littering the fields with their dead and wounded. "The whole landscape for an instant turned red," one northern soldier later wrote. Another veteran recalled, "[The cornfield] was so full of bodies that a man could have walked through it without stepping on the ground." No clear victor emerged and the fighting stopped out of sheer exhaustion. Lee withdrew during the night of September 18, and re-crossed the Potomac. Tactically, the battle ended in a draw. Strategically, it was a victory for the Union.

This battle almost speaks for itself in illustrating the gruesomeness of the human condition. All manner of explanations have been offered for the origin of the War Between the States: slavery, states rights, the right of secession, a conspiracy to break up the Republic, etc. In a day's time, horrific death was strewn all across this battlefield—the lowly cornfield being the site where so many young soldiers fell. If it is true that "the grave cannot praise you," then one wonders why God continually lets men engage in activities whose ultimate outcome is the inability to praise him. "Does anyone know where the love of God goes when the waves turn the minutes to hours?" wrote Gordon Lightfoot concerning a seafaring disaster known as the wreck of the Edmond Fitzgerald. Mankind has asked this question in one form or another repeatedly since the beginning.

So where was God on September 16–18, 1862 during the bloodiest days in American history when the soldiers on both sides of this battle needed him so desperately? I suspect if the truth were known, one of the reasons why Christians are ridiculed—perhaps even hated—so passionately by some is because we hold onto the belief that God provides providential care—even in the face of so much evidence that suggests otherwise.

And while it is certainly true that men have busily been killing themselves since the time of Cain, this earth, biosphere, mother-nature—or whatever you want to call it—is responsible for taking a lot of human life, too. It is amazing how lethal gravity and trees are. Usually, the year doesn't go by that I won't hear a story about some poor soul who decided to climb a mountain, and along the way, loses his or her footing and ends up falling 1000 feet or more to their death. I've also heard of another person who loved skiing, and while tossing a football at the same time, forgot to look out for oncoming traffic—in this case, an oncoming tree. On December 31, 1997, Michael Kennedy, who was the sixth of eleven children of Robert F. Kennedy and Ethel Skakel, learned that lesson the hard way. And less than a week later, Republican Congressman Sonny Bono also died in a skiing accident. But deaths from these causes are relatively rare. When people think of the threats and nature, they usually think of things like hurricanes, tornadoes, earthquakes—with very good reason.

THE ROLE OF NATURAL EVENTS —NEVADO DEL RUIZ

The village of Armero died on November 13, 1985, or more correctly, the people who lived in that village died. They had the misfortune of living on the slopes of an ancient volcano—Nevado del Ruiz. This volcano—the second highest in the Northern Hemisphere—is located in the Andes mountain range in the country of Colombia. Nevado del Ruiz's height guarantees that its peak remains covered in deep snow. That is, it remains covered in snow until an eruption occurs. The last eruption occurred in 1595—well beyond the memory trace of anyone living in 1985. The vulcanologists tried to warn government officials that an eruption was imminent but were ignored—until it was too late. The eruption from Ruiz's summit crater occurred on November 13, 1985, at 9:08pm huge portions of the 25,000 square kilometers of snow instantly turned into millions of tons of water and picked up speed and debris as it moved down the mountain. The phenomenon created by such eruptions is called a Lahar. Lahars have the consistency of "freshly made concrete." So millions of metric tons, the consistency of wet, fresh concrete, bore down on the sleeping village of Armero at up to sixty kilometers per hour. This freight train swept the village of Armero away and passed its citizens into death in much the same way a broom turns out dust. Twenty-three thousand people started perishing after 11:00 pm. This amounted to almost 80 percent of Armero's 28,700 residents. Once again, this is just another of the thousands of events that have occurred—and will continue to occur—that consume the lives of men and women. And while we can expect nature to be unpredictable, should we have a slightly better expectation of a God who says he loves all mankind? How can we begin to explain such seeming indifference on the part of God—a being that professes love for all his creatures—as he sits idly by watching nature so indiscriminately take the lives of so many?

THE ROLE OF NATURAL EVENTS—THE TSUNAMI OF 2004

The island of Sumatra sits on the eastern coast of the Indian Ocean. Thanks to 24-hour news channels, events on the opposite side of the planet are just a push button away for review. So it was on December 26, 2004 that within a few hours after a 9.2 magnitude earthquake struck off the northwest coast of the island of Sumatra, the western world knew about it. A thirty-foot displacement in the ocean floor set in motion a monstrous tsunami that radiated outward in all directions. Just north of the epicenter, several small islands disappeared completely. The waves kept traveling arriving in Sumatra, Sri Lanka, Indonesia, Thailand, India and even Somalia on the east coast of Africa. Sri Lanka alone lost 31,000 people. These people were just a part of the estimated overall death toll of 240,000–250,000. No one really knows for sure how many people died that day. It was not long before articles sprang up in newspapers, blogs and websites with people trying to explain why God would allow such monstrous destruction to occur. Even Muslim clerics weighed in and tried to explain the tsunami. One such cleric said the tsunami was the result of Allah's displeasure with the sex tourism industry in that part of the world.

The destruction of Armero affected mainly Roman Catholic believers. The people living in the area where this tsunami occurred are largely Hindu, Buddhist, and Muslim. So, apparently, God is no respecter of religion when it comes to meting out disaster, but that is hardly a reason to praise or worship him. And just because most of them were not Christian, is that any justification for God to destroy them? Were not many of those killed, nonetheless, people who prayed? What good did prayer do for these quarter-million dead? Or had they done things which forced God in his awful justice and holy wrath to unceremoniously sweep them all away? Just who is this God of heaven? If God wanted Christianity to spread into that area of the world with its fundamental message of a loving—and supposedly providential—God, is inflicting a tsunami on the people who lived there the best introduction He could have come up with?

After examining only a handful of recorded—and even non-recorded events, for surely we could have added many, many more and we are equally sure you could add many of your own—I hope the reader will at least agree that if there is an answer or explanation as to why God causes or allows such horrific events as these to happen, that it had better be more meaningful than the usual, "Well, God's ways are too mysterious for us to understand." That's not much of an answer when the cold, hard reality is that in his absence, benign neglect or outright hostility, every year millions of people around the world simply cease to exist. For all the biblical assertions and televangelist sermonizing to the contrary, his loving care for most if not all of the people on this planet doesn't seem to amount to much, if any at all. I mention the appeal to "mysteries-of-God" answer because more than once, when we have pressed our fellow believers about these issues, they eventually run for the hills, claim ignorance and hide behind this mantra. We are told this, as if this is actually supposed to comfort us, and we are expected to treat it as a genuine answer to our questions. The fact is such a response is meant to shut down discussion, investigation and communication rather than to make a serious attempt to address these issues.

In our brief classification of the ways the loss of life is routinely suffered on this planet, we were so busy focusing on answering the questions "Where is he when bad things happen?" and "Why doesn't he do anything about them?" that we completely overlooked the possibility of gaining useful information into God's actions—or rather his inactions—by asking a related, but slightly different question, "What would it have meant for God to intervene in these and other horrific events if he had done so openly?" Perhaps in answering that question, we can gain new insight into answering the original questions.

The nature of the original questions we asked is based on the observed reality that God rarely openly reveals himself when such disasters occur. Why? So if for some reason, God has determined that he must remain in the background during human activity, then we can ask what it would have meant for God to act openly at Pearl Harbor.

To prevent the horrific loss of life at Pearl Harbor, God would have had to stop the accurate targeting of the *Arizona*. That would have been easy enough for him to accomplish unobserved, but what about the fate of the men on the *West Virginia* or *Oklahoma*? The idea that twenty torpedo bombers were going to miss these stationary behemoths is just not plausible. And once the raid was over, God would have had to liquefy metal to allow the men trapped in the ships to escape. Certainly, he could have done so, but *not* without being noticed. Can you imagine the newspaper headlines that would have streamed from that day forward? "PROOF GOD EXISTS! Miracle in Hawaii—How doomed men were delivered from certain death." And how could he have stopped the Japanese Zeroes from being able to shoot down the planes of VT-3, VT-6, and VT-8? Further, short of changing the characteristics of matter, how could God have stopped the barrage of AAA hurled up from the ground as the B-17s flew overhead? And how do you openly stop men from killing each other if they're determined to do so?

To prevent the carnage at Stalingrad all God would have to have done is to snuff out the lives of two fleas—Stalin and Hitler. Poof, problem solved! Surely a Divine elimination policy enacted across the centuries against all would-be tyrants would make this world a much better place to live. But, then, why not just get rid of all evil people? After all, surely he knows which of us are "really evil" and have aspirations to global conquest. That's got to be a relatively small number of miscreants. Why not just arrange a proper set of aneurisms, heart attacks, cancers, the odd lightning strike and be done with it? God could certainly do such things yet I have to think it would still be very difficult for him to do such things without being noticed.

The War Between the States—a national tragedy if ever there was one—must have been a preventable war. Surely our God has the kind of power to prevent Christian people from warring with one another, right? A simple dream, burning bush or a voice from Heaven to Jefferson Davis—or Lincoln—and the problem would have been solved. No questions asked. Or God could have sent a stand down order to every soldier on both sides of the conflict had he chosen to do so, but could he have done so without being noticed?

Scientists have tried in vain to predict the moment when the next earthquake will hit or when the next volcano will erupt. Surely God knows the timing of these rare events. The Earth, while habitable, is hardly a friendly biosphere. Floods, tornadoes, typhoons, hurricanes, earthquakes and eruptions will continue to take human life so long as this planet's current configuration remains unchanged. If Robert Redford can be a horse-whisperer, surely God can pick a volcano-whisperer every now and then. With just such an advanced warning that he alone could have provided, the death toll of December 26, 2004 could have been greatly reduced, perhaps even eliminated. Ditto for Monday, August 27, 1883—the day when Mount Krakatoa blew up off the coast of Indonesia, once known as Java, and November 13, 1985—or any other date which became noteworthy because of a man-made or natural disaster. The question remains whether God could have alerted mankind without exposing himself.

So the results seem to be mixed. Perhaps God could have done some of these things without revealing himself but it also seems highly likely that there are many things that he could not intervene in without doing so openly. Would that have been so bad? Why is it so important that God stay in the background? As we listed above, at least for us, four reasons come to mind. :

First, human behavior would change dramatically if it ever became widely known that God exists – but not for the right reasons. Have you ever watched driver reaction when a possible traffic hazard arises, or when someone has become aware that a highway patrolman is nearby and monitoring speed by use of radar? It has been our experience that everyone slows down when they think such a threat is nearby. Why? The answer is obvious—the risk of financial threat or possible loss of liberty forces people to modify their behavior. Notice I said forces. If people were happy to drive the speed limit, there would be no need to alter, let alone monitor their behavior. It has also been our experience that once everyone thinks the threat has passed, we have generally noticed an immediate return to the speed the drivers had been cruising at before they became aware of the threat.

Now, why is that? Notice the imposition of change on driver behavior via threat is usually short-lived because the threat, no matter how mild or severe, is unable to change the heart of the driver. Further, we suspect that the reaction to the presence of a speed-trap is one of anger, not appreciation, because the human condition is such that it generally resents being told to do anything. And if humans have to be forced to obey rules and laws as mundane as speed limits, it should not come as too much of a surprise to see what sanctions are necessary to prevent people from engaging in much more dangerous and evil behavior.

So if you expand this line of reasoning, it shouldn't take a person very long to see why God must remain in the background during this present evil age. Should proof of his existence become an incontrovertible fact and known to all the peoples of the Earth, how long do you think it would be before people would "start behaving" in a way similar to the drivers we just described? How long would it be before they curbed their actions out of fear and not because they believed that they should behave a certain way because it was for the best? And what good is freedom when it's compulsory? What good is it to be forced to act a certain way when you have no desire to or when you internally desire to behave differently? We could celebrate that the amount of criminal activity would practically drop to zero, but it would be for the wrong reasons. Living life a certain way only to avoid punishment is no way to live at all. And we have no doubt that God does not want people to guard their behavior only because they wish to avoid being punished for their sins. God wants people to live righteously because it's the right thing to do.

God has no interest in forcing behavior because force is incompatible with the freedom he longs to give us all. God has no interest in building robots. So it becomes necessary—and always has been—for God to remain in the background while he waits for people in every generation to convince themselves that behaving for the right reasons really is the right and best thing to do. And not just because of force or the threat of punishment.

Secondly, if he were to openly intervene, the possibility of learning many of life's most important lessons —whether small or large—would be rendered practically impossible. This one is also a universal lesson—it is simply for a person to learn just who they really are away from the glare of the spotlight. But it is only because men and women now feel free to act that our real character—or the lack of it—is expressed. Nobody likes to learn while someone's looking over their shoulder. But God knows that.

Every day trillions of actions are taken and trillions of decisions have to be made which result in those actions. Yes, it would be amazing and truly wonderful if all those decisions were good decisions, but the reality is, they aren't. I've always been amazed at hearing people being interviewed after they've made mistakes in the past, say things like, "if I had only known then what I know now, I never would have done. . ." and they proceed to describe whatever it was that they now wish they had done differently. Poignantly, I am thinking at this moment of the great actor Yul Brynner who made a commercial—I think it was for the American Cancer Society—warning people that he wished he had never smoked and that if he had never smoked he would not be suffering from the cancer which eventually took his life. Some lessons we learn about ourselves are very, very expensive indeed! And for every publicly professed reflection, there well may be 10,000 more that aren't—but they are nonetheless experienced every moment everywhere throughout the entire world and in every moment, people are learning something about themselves—things, both good and bad.

War is evil. On the one hand, soldiers from all nations have done the most monstrous of things—raping, pillaging and slaughtering the defenseless. On the other hand, soldiers in every generation have had to learn to face their worst fears and overcome them. Some soldiers have nobly sacrificed themselves for the lives of their fellow soldiers. As horrific as war is, is there any doubt that these soldiers throughout the centuries have had to learn things about themselves that they might not otherwise have learned? (Please understand me here—I am not arguing at all for the use of war to train people. But the fact that wars exist, it seems to me, is an indictment of the human condition. Sadly, I think it is an extension of the lack of goodwill that haunts the hearts of so many people. And silently, over in the corner of the room perhaps, sit many closed and neglected Bibles—and every one of them would tell its readers that God wants man to love their neighbors as themselves.)

Wars don't happen in a vacuum, do they? Over the years, I've read many of the historical accounts concerning the battles in World War II. It is amazing in how many ways people were affected by that and subsequent wars. My dad ended up being injured during the war—because of a wet floor at the Army base where he was stationed. One night as he left the showers, he slipped and fell on the small of his back. I am sure he did not realize it at the time, but that injury was the start of progressive arthritis which sat in and followed him to his death at the age of fifty-nine. So in effect, his injury was caused because God allowed—or was it because he placed—Adolf Hitler in control of Germany. I am not making a comparison between my losses and the horrific losses so many other people suffered during World War II—and yet his injury did affect his life, and therefore mine. (Yes, I know, he could just as easily have been injured in some other accident around the house as well even if there wasn't a war.) I'm only illustrating that there were many consequences—many which never made the news and only the individual would know about. "What the hell was God thinking?" I often asked myself when I was younger. Surely God—if he is truly omniscient—would've known what a monster Hitler would end up being and how many lives he would be responsible for taking. Why didn't God "exterminate him?"

Of course, if God got rid of all such dictators, tyrants, and despots, the world would never have known to what depths mankind has "fallen" or just what acts of barbarism we are capable of committing with the limited freedom he has given us. People need to remember that Hitler didn't cause the deaths of 50 million people by himself. Generals to privates—soldiers and civilians carrying out his orders generated the death toll of WWII. Further, Germany entered into alliances with Japan and Italy. Those agreements increased the scope of death into other areas around the world. Whether in Africa, the Pacific or in Europe, individuals had to make choices everyday—whether to do good or evil. We know the outcome. Many chose to do evil and preserve their lives. And so the killing went on. Every wrong decision added to the horror of the war in its own way. But every man's morality and conscience were tested by the events of that war.

I argue that human behavior would likely change drastically if knowledge of God's existence became universally and incontrovertibly known. No more war! Hurray! (The world might-well become crime free, especially if the endless sermons concerning the wrath of God became the most-heard type of sermon). Strike up the band! The world would become the Utopia that dreamers in so many ages have longed for the world to be. And that brings us to the third reason why it is likely imperative that God's existence remains subject to debate.

By immersing the human condition in evil, God is reflexively creating the desire for the eventual destruction of evil by generating an overpowering desire for goodness. Can you seriously imagine such a world—a world without war? Probably not. It is often with a sad shrug of the shoulders that when asked how they would fix this world, that a person is rendered speechless. There's just too much that's broke down here. But it is the fact that we all "know" just how horrible this crime-ridden world is that makes dreaming of a crime free world such a utopian desire.

Make no mistake about it, things really are that rough. We've only documented a handful of the millions of events that provide the evidence which proves this fact. This world's character is born of a genuine reality. Yet, quietly, almost imperceptibly, the cumulative effect of evil in all of its forms is that it plants seeds which grow into a sincere and burning desire for things to get better.

It is the very essence of this age's evil character that makes us appreciate and hunger for things to get better. There is another way to look at this issue by asking the following question, "Would mankind earnestly long for things to get better if things weren't as bad as they are?"

At a more fundamental level, there is something rather unseemly about people whose only motivation for walking righteously is out of fear of punishment—that is because of force. Instead, God wants us to learn to act out of love—always—and until we can, we are not ready to inherit the power that comes with his image and likeness. And this brings us to our final reason why we are convinced that God must stay in the background during mankind's existence upon this earth, and it is in our estimation, the most important reason which necessitates God remaining hidden is: God has set a goal for himself, which is to make man into his image and likeness, a goal which is mentioned in the first pages of the book of Genesis. Our faith is based on the fact that we've seen nothing biblically or historically to make us believe he has changed his mind about this goal. Indeed, Colossians 1:12–14 and John 1:7 still read respectively as they have for over 1900 years. My paraphrase:

> Giving thanks to the Father, the One who has qualified us to share in the inheritance of the saints in the light, who rescued us out of the authority of darkness and translated us into the Kingdom of his beloved Son, in whom, we now have our redemption, even the forgiveness of sins.

Here, one of the many reasons believers—and ultimately all people so far as we are concerned—should be thankful to God and happy to express gratitude to God is for two reasons: first, because he qualified us to be partakers of his inheritance in the saints, bathed in eternal light; and second, because he rescued us from the power of darkness, translating us into the Kingdom of his beloved Son.

Many would object that this description is only for believers. Yet, John—when speaking of this same light—assures us all that the reason Jesus came is so that *all* will believe through him: "He came for a testimony, in order that he should testify concerning the light, in order that all should come to believe through him." In *Robertson's Word Pictures* author A. T. Robertson affirms our translation is correct, though he says nothing about the implication of the adjective, *all*.

The difference between us and too many of our fellow believers is that we are willing to give God the benefit of the doubt here. He said *all*—and we believe he meant it. One day *all* are to believe! All are to be translated from the power of darkness into the Kingdom of Light—the Kingdom of his beloved Son. We don't know when—but we are convinced that he is able—because he really is all-powerful. (Anyone who can make a universe from scratch has power beyond human capacity to fully apprehend. So we take it by faith.) And we are willing to believe that if he didn't want to make us in his image, he wouldn't have said it! The declaration is universal because we think God's heart is universal and so is his plan for mankind. His plan is a reflection of *His image*!

But just what is his image? What is he like? We could write a book on this topic alone. The full appreciation of his image is beyond the scope of this book. Although his image may have many characteristics, if we were to boil it down to just three, we would say:

1. He is free to act as he pleases
2. He is powerful because he possesses all knowledge
3. He is love and his actions are always motivated by it

God is totally free and powerful, and he desires you and me to be like him. But it is more than mere desire. It is our destiny to become like him. One of these days, we are going to be like Jesus. If it takes 70–100 years of struggle, suffering and training so that I can be an eternal agent of good, then sign me up!

SOME ENCOURAGEMENT — THE BIBLICAL VIEW OF THIS AGE

It will probably come as a surprise to the reader to know the Bible already has addressed these issues, but not in the way perhaps we would have liked. In one brief teaching Jesus covered the acts of men, nature and personal experience and how we should view the question of fairness as it relates to this present evil age. Consider the following passage, Luke 13:1–5:

> Now there were some present at that time who told Jesus about the Galileans whose blood Pilate had mixed with their sacrifices. Jesus answered,'Do you think that these Galileans were worse sinners than all the other Galileans because they suffered this way? I tell you, no! But unless you repent, you too will all perish. Or those eighteen who died when the tower in Siloam fell on them—do you think they were guiltier than all the others living in Jerusalem? I tell you, no! But unless you repent, you too will all perish.' (NIV)

Jesus relates a contemporaneous event in which Pilate mixed the blood of some people with their own sacrifices. In a word, ouch! This example can typify all man made events. Although the cause, which knocked down the tower, is not specified, it is not unreasonable to conclude that an earthquake or storm may have played the role of cause. If so, this can typify all natural or "acts of God" type events. And of course, both of these events would have had personal effects to the people affected by these events. In any event, Jesus teaches that the source of the unfairness or evil is not really the issue—what we do about him is. Jesus tells men to repent. I've heard more hand-wringing sermons about "true repentance" than I would care to count. I have no problem accepting what the fundamental components of the word in Greek say they mean. Repentance to Jesus was simply meta-noeoo, which means to change the mind. We will all repent. Some will do so before others. Those who seek salvation are required to do so now. The legions of the lost will change their minds once they are ushered into his presence on Judgment day. Jesus does not deny that horrible things will happen; he just wants us to be aware that knowing him is more important than knowing why such events happen.

LUKE 9:23-27; THE COST OF DISCIPLESHIP— CARRYING YOUR CROSS

> And he said to all, "If anyone would come after me, let him deny himself and take up his cross daily and follow me. Forwhoever would save his life will lose it, but whoever loses his life for my sake will save it. For what does it profit a man if he gains the whole world and loses or forfeits himself? For whoever is ashamed of me and of my words, of him will the Son of Man be ashamed when he comes in his glory and the glory of the Father and of the holy angels. But I tell you truly, there are some standing here who will not taste death until they see the kingdom of God.' (ESV)

Following the Lord has never been easy. In fact, following Christ is a form of daily death. At the very minimum, it requires a willingness to put Godly pursuits ahead of individual ones. Our service can run the gamut from giving someone who is thirsty something to drink, to feeding the hungry on one end, to the actual laying down of our lives at the other. Hence, we are to have the willingness to provide the smallest kindness to being willing to die in his name. This is just part of what it means to his servant. Only a servant who has emptied his own desires can serve the Lord by the "cross"—that is to the point of death. In other words, only a servant committed to the point of death will be able to be a servant of the Lord. Committing to be his servant, a servant of all—that is what it means to act in love. This is the character of God and this is what he is training us to be like. Although God cares about us, he is unable to lift the requirement recorded in Luke: we have a cross to bear. It is in those situations when we find ourselves in the uncomfortable gap between our circumstances and his inability to help us without exposing his existence that we need to remember what we signed on for when he called us: death. It is a sobering call to be a servant of Christ. We should not abandon the Lord when we find ourselves, seemingly, abandoned by him. It was part of the assignment, part of the training, and we should face that fact squarely—before the dark days come. We should decide before circumstances in the valley arrive that we are going to stick with him—no matter what the cost. Romans 8:35–39:

> Who shall separate us from the love of Christ? Shall trouble or hardship or persecution or famine or nakedness or danger or sword? As it is written, 'For your sake we face death all day long; we are considered as sheep to be slaughtered.' No, in all these things we are more than conquerors through him who loved us. For I am convinced that neither death nor life, neither angels, nor demons, neither the present, nor the future, nor any powers, neither height, nor depth, nor anything else in all creation, will be able to separate us from the love of God that is in Christ Jesus our Lord. (NIV)

There are many promises in the Bible. To my estimation, this is the only one that matters, at least insofar as our current walk and this age is concerned. Look at that this list of obstacles Paul articulates. If it were true that being in God freed us from such dangers, as some people incorrectly believe, then one would be hard pressed to understand why Paul asserts that we should expect these realities to be a part of our walk. The most important point of this teaching is that our circumstances in life do not change God's love for us.

You say you're broke and impoverished. He still loves you. He is still with you. Life is has become unbearably hard. He still loves you. He is still with you. You face being beheaded for your love of Christ. He still loves you. He is still with you. You've lost your job, home, family or facing a deadly disease. He still loves you. He is still with you. You face the sword—death in any number of ways. He still loves you. He is still with you. You're experiencing a painful and chronic disease. He still loves you. He is still with you.

Paul maintains, "We are more than conquerors through him who loved us." In fact, facing slaughter all the daylong is part of the experience we will encounter in one form or another during our journey here. It still doesn't matter: his love for us changes not. His plans for us are great. The finished product is what he is after and what he will achieve—perfection in us. But never lose sight of this fact—he is still with you.

If this teaching ever truly penetrates to the core of our beings, we will find the power to carry on in our service of him. Once we stop judging God's love for us by our circumstances, we will become much more effective servants. It is so easy to ask. "Lord, if you really love me, then why has all this disaster befallen me?" The answer is no more complex than this: he still loves you even in the middle of your circumstance—whether he put you in the circumstance or you put yourself in it. God did not single out the men on the *West Virginia* for a gruesome extermination because he no longer loved them. God did not stop loving the men on the *Arizona* either before or after their deaths. God does not stop loving those who are swept away by lahars, tsunamis, wars or any other disaster, man-made or natural. It is also why I know that my dad, my mom and the experiences and trials I have yet to undergo—no matter how evil—will not change his love for me! His love remains constant as the sun. His course remains steady. His plan for the future of mankind and our eternal destiny remains unchanged by the hectic and ever changing circumstances we face on Earth. Once we understand this fact, perhaps we can understand why the circumstances of our life really don't matter—at least with respect to his love for us and our eternal destiny.

Does this mean God will not intervene in your life? If his past dealings are any indication, most of the time, he is not likely to—at least, openly. If he does, you should count yourself extremely blessed. Whether he acts on your behalf in a way you can realize or not, you can be sure of one thing: his love for you remains constant and eternal. Is God still working behind the scenes? I can't prove it, but I certainly believe he is. But he is far too subtle and smart in his efforts for anyone as blind and clumsy as I to detect his actions. It seems to me that Inspector Clouseau would have better luck catching the Pink Panther than for any person to find out what God has or has not done on any given day. Just how smart is God?

Well, another piece of evidence that has only recently come to my attention suggests just how smart he is. There are few preachers who will sincerely preach the grace of God in all of its glory and kindness. Joseph Prince is one such pastor. In lesson number 144 (Healing Through God's Gift of Righteousness—Part 2 of 3), he told his audience that he has a very unique understanding to a two letter combination of Hebrew letters—the *Aleph* and the *Tav* found at various locations throughout the Hebrew scriptures, for example, Genesis 1:1. For thousands of years no one has been able to assign a meaning to this two letter combination because there is nothing in the Hebrew language or its vocabulary that matches it. It's not a word. So it has remained a confusing set of markings that are part of the historical record—until now. Pastor Prince discovered—or was a revelation from God?—the meaning of these two letters. God, he discovered, had hidden the meaning of this letter combination, choosing only to reveal its meaning when the writers of the New Testament wrote the documents that were eventually assembled as the New Testament. Specifically, the book of Revelation provides the key to understanding this two-letter enigma.

Pastor Prince quoted the verse in which Jesus Christ claimed that he is the Alpha and Omega—the Beginning and the End, the First and the Last. Alpha and Omega are the first and last letters of the Greek language. But what of Aleph and Tav? Well it turns out that these two letters are the first and last letters of the Hebrew language! So thousands of years before Jesus Christ appeared, God had already written his name, his Son's name on the Old Testament! (This is a reasonable interpretation because the Greek language was used to translate the Hebrew scriptures (the LXX). And he hid it in plain sight. Amazingly, the descendants of Israel to this day do not know about this revelation because they have no use for the New Testament in general and the book of Revelation in particular. Only believers in Christ have the key to understanding this riddle. And God graciously gave the key to one of the writers of the New Testament. But it was there all along. The meaning was there all along—but no one could see it. But it was there.

Now the reason I tell you this story is to assert the idea that God is not only loving and kind—but that he has been here all along—hidden from our eyes, but nonetheless here. Although we long to see him in plain sight, we are called to trust that even though we don't see him now—he, like the meaning of those two letters—has been here all along. That is how brilliant God is.

But for now, this is the world's reality—Romans 8:20–23:

> For the creation itself was subjected to frustration, not by its own choice, but by the will of the one who subjected it, in hope that the creation itself will be liberated from its bondage to decay and brought into the glorious freedom of the children of God. We know that the whole creation has been groaning as in the pains of child birthright up to the present time. Not only so, but we ourselves, who have the first fruits of the Spirit, groan inwardly as we wait eagerly for our adoption as sons, the redemption of our bodies. (NIV)

The Brightness around Him

Before I finish my thoughts I thought I would leave the reader with my personal observations by returning to the opening description of the loss of my parents and how it affected me in light of the guidance I included above. What did I learn from those tragically sad events in light of these criteria?

First, I accept the idea that every human—myself included—would behave differently than I desired if God's existence were an incontrovertible fact—even if I don't know for sure how it would have changed. But would I behave because I loved him or because I feared for my eternal destiny?

Second, I often wonder what lessons I would have missed learning if God had miraculously healed my parents. Would I be quite as sure that humility is the currency of eternity? I don't think so. Would I have experienced "survivor's guilt" when others lost their loved ones? I would think that that is highly likely. And would I have been able to empathize with others when they faced the grief of loss? I don't think so.

Third, and obviously, I can only speak for myself, but I have developed an intense hatred of the evil that infests this planet—and you cannot imagine how depressing it is for me to confront the reality that I contribute to the evil that occurs on this planet—by just being alive. As Paul said, sin lives in my members—just like it does in everyone else. My failures haunt me—and I suspect the lives of millions of others. Yet God gave me the freedom to learn this and many other truths without looking over my shoulder. He does the same for everyone else as well. But would I have acquired the abhorrence of evil if it wasn't such a pervasive and gut-wrenching reality? Once again, I think not.

Fourth, to a certain degree, my responses—including the one for this item—are based on faith. To me it is an article of faith that God would be prevented from achieving his ultimate goal of making mankind into the image of his beloved Son, if he did not make this environment the way it is. That he would have done things differently if he could have, I attribute to his goodness—which is yet, another article of faith for me. Somewhere along the way, though, I've learned the lack of proof of his existence is what makes it possible for people to actually exercise their faith. And again, because of his good will and kindness, I have every reason to believe that he will honor those who came to trust in him—both his existence and his goodness.

But that brings us full circle, doesn't it? Ultimately, I will see my parents again. For now, though, I will have to content myself with the memories of them and all the joy that brings. I *believe* he will keep his word. I *trust* that he will honor his word. And that, it turns out, is because this is the God that I've come to know over these many years. And should I ever be asked, "Who do you say

Beyond This Moment

Jesus Christ is?"—as Jesus did so many centuries ago (Matthew 16), my answer would be a reflection of all the things I've learned along the way. Since I know how I would answer this question, out of curiosity, I wonder how each reader would answer this question: Who do you say Jesus Christ is? And would your answer be different—if you knew he actually existed?

And that was the conclusion of Mike's article. All I can say is I sincerely appreciate his perspective and hope you do too. He has given us something to consider while observing life under the microscope of the present. His story and experiences are probably closer to most than mine, and I hope you can see why I admire the work God has done in his life.

Mike and I have spent hours upon hours over the past several years asking ourselves why God subjects us to so much stress and frustration in this life. We both arrived at the same conclusion, although he did so much sooner than me: There is no other way to bring free-will agents to perfection.

God places a tremendous value on freedom and liberty, and it is not surprising that the greatest civilizations on earth are the ones who have allowed them to flourish. But before he gives us the type of freedom and power that he enjoys, he has to make sure we are mature enough to handle these great gifts responsibly. The classroom environment for our training demands universal ambiguity and that ambivalence ultimately deepens our freedom.

He has a plan, and it's a good one. Whether we agree with him or not, he will not stop until we are made complete in his image. In summary, the training to bring his children into maturity is a necessity to him, even though to us, it may at times be unclear, unwanted, unattractive, and appearing as arbitrary and exclusive. "Why is this happening to me?" But the end result of our development is obvious, compelling, beautiful, deliberate, and most importantly, inclusive, because God so loved the world.

10

BLOOM

~

For many years I was perplexed by a statement made by Paul to the Corinthians about being caught up to the third heaven. In this chapter I'm going to insert what I recently learned about it, because it is so relevant to what we have discussed in this book so far.

Have you ever asked yourself, "Why three heavens?" Wouldn't one be good enough? Thinking spatially, in the past I wondered if they were stacked on top of each other and if there were other heavens even higher? I had other questions too, some serious—like what differentiates one from another—and some not so serious—like is the food better in the third heaven? How about jobs or the housing market? Do we receive better health care coverage as we progress upward? Or maybe Jesus lives in the upper heavens with God in the penthouse and only visits the lower levels occasionally; I don't know. I just hope the golf courses are comparable because my sin handicap is probably far too high to ever qualify for playing at the next level.

Most of these are rather silly questions to ponder, and I've used a few of them sarcastically in conversations with others to divert attention away from my complete ignorance on the subject. Still, I wondered about some of them occasionally until a few days ago when it occurred to me that you can't improve on perfection any more than you can multiply infinitely by two or three and get a larger number. This realization opened the door of understanding and tied together several other scriptures that I was previously unsure about.

So just what makes these three heavens different? I believe the answer is so simple. The only difference is the number of people residing there at three different points in time. Let me explain. In my view Paul informs us in an earlier letter to the Corinthians that all people will be brought to perfection in one of three groups, "each man in his own order." The mention of a third heaven was about timing and it had nothing to do with space. As a matter of fact, the Greek word translated *"to"* in the phrase "caught up *to* the third heaven" actually means *unto* or *until* as in James 5:7 ". . . be patient . . . *until* the coming of the Lord." Simply put, the third heaven is the same perfect place as the first one, just later in time with more people in it.

I am now convinced that Paul was caught up to a time after the third harvest of people when everyone had finally arrived in paradise and God had become all in all. It was a vision of a fully populated heaven. One can argue about the size of the first two heavens, but in Paul's vision, the work of Christ had been finished, all of the training had been completed, all of the graves had been emptied, all men had been given life, and death had finally been abolished.

What follows is some potential insight into these three groups and our Father's great plan to redeem all. It comes from a passage in 1 Corinthians. Dr. Stephen Jones in his book *Creation's Jubilee* stirred my interest in this subject and I highly recommend reading his perspective. It's difficult, or nearly impossible to see the great news in these verses given our modern translations, but a few additional insights opened my to the three groups, three major feast celebrations, three major harvests, three main crops, three resurrections, and consequently, three views of heaven at three different points in time.

The following is found in 1 Cor 15:22–28:

> For as in Adam all die, even so in Christ all shall be made alive. But each one in his own order: Christ the firstfruits, afterwards, those who are Christ's at his coming. Then comes the end, when he delivers the kingdom to God the Father, when he puts an end to all rule and authority and power. For he must reign until he has put all enemies under his feet. The last enemy that will be destroyed is death. For he has put all things under his feet. But when he says 'all things are put under him,' it is evident that he who put all things under him is excepted. Now when all things are made subject to him, the Son himself will also be subject to him who put all things under him, that God may be all in all.

After having established Christ as the first one to be resurrected prior to verse twenty-two, Paul begins a discussion on how all others will be vivified. *Tagma* is the word translated as "order" in verse twenty-three, and it is a military word signifying a company, or squadron. I've also seen the word "set" used. So each individual will be placed in one of the squadrons as spelled out in the remainder of verse twenty-three and into twenty-four.

First, a commentary on verse twenty-two: I've read and heard all kinds of explanations, and it is very bizarre to me how those with the more traditional view try to work around what seems obvious. Death through Adam is universal and Paul draws a parallel where vivification through Christ will be just as ubiquitous.

Back to *tagma*. The first squadron in the list is normally translated as "Christ the firstfruits" and most believe this strictly refers to Jesus. However, Dr. Jones explains how others see the possibility that this group could be called "anointed firstfruits." I like his rationale. From the words of Paul, we are looking for squadrons of men, and one individual does not make a squadron. Also, *christos* in the Greek means anointed. Put an article in front of it, and you have "the anointed," or "the Christ" as in verses twenty-two and twenty-three immediately above and below. However, the article is not found in this part of the verse, meaning "anointed" is indefinite and could refer to any man, any group of men, or anything(s) anointed. In the LXX—the Greek translation of the Hebrew scriptures also known as the Septuagint—for example, Exodus 29:29 refers to unleavened loaves anointed with oil. This verb is spelled *christheenai* showing that the noun and verb are linked in meaning. In summary, since the introduction to verse twenty-three references a company of people, I believe the possibility exists that the anointed here refers to a squadron of men called firstfruits.

Some may still want to argue that the first group should be called "Christ the firstfruits, " because a quick check in Corinthians reveals that *christos* does not always have an article in front of it when referring to Christ. Paul places the article in front of christos about half of the time. Maybe there is some grammatical reason for what appears to be inconsistent, or maybe the Holy Spirit left it ambiguous so that we could have this discussion. But Dr. Jones' point above is still a valid one and we can clearly see his thought process.

I believe we can find common ground if we view Christ symbolically as a many-membered body and the firstfruits as a special group within that body. I say special in that they are harvested first among all believers with the rest of them coming with the second squadron, "those that are with him at his coming." The NIV refers to this second group as "those who belong to him" at the time of his appearance as opposed to those who do not.

Another possibility exists in naming the first squadron as simply "firstfruits." Since the entire passage begins and ends with the idea that all men are "in Christ," it follows that all of the squadrons listed come under the heading of "Christ." After all, Jesus did take on our identity and our debt on the cross. Paul's main argument in this entire passage is that since Christ has been vivified, and since we are all in him, then all of humanity will also be vivified.

Mathematically, I see a set of one named "Christ" being broken down into three subsets. Using this line of reasoning, and since there is no punctuation in the Greek manuscript, one can take the liberty and add a colon after "Christ" and then begin naming the list of subsets within Christ. The first subset is the firstfruits of the believers, and the second is the rest of the believers. Personally, I lean toward this point of view, although I would not argue with anyone over the other two interpretations.

Concerning the second group, I also see the possibility that it will be much larger than what we may have believed in the past. Personally, I think a better translation identifies the second group as "those who are Christ's in His presence" as the Concordant Literal New Testament renders it. So who will be Christ's in His presence? To me, these are people who have already accepted Him, or ones whose hearts have been prepared to bow and worship Him when they see Him face to face. This group includes Gandhi and others who had not been given the gift of faith previously. In humility, they repent and swear the oath found in Isaiah when they realize what He has done for them. They become His in His presence or at His coming, not necessarily before, and from that point forward, they forever belong to Him. As someone who has been in His presence, I can easily see how His love will instantly melt their hearts.

I also believe the Feast of Trumpets points directly at these two groups. God told Moses to make two silver trumpets to be used to summon his people. When one trumpet blew, only the leaders of the people were to gather, but when two were blown, it meant all of God's people were to respond. Later, God said these trumpets should be blown on "the day of your gladness" and would serve as a reminder "of you (standing) before your God." So Israel blew the trumpets on an autumn festival called the Feast of Trumpets, also called the Day of the Awakening Blast.

Revelation 20:4–6 also speaks of two resurrections and commends those who achieve the first one:

> And I saw the souls of those who had been beheaded because of the testimony of Jesus and because of the word of God, and those who had not worshipped the beast or his image, and had not received the mark on their forehead and upon their hand: and they came to life and reigned with Christ for a thousand years. The rest of the dead did not come to life until the thousand years were completed. Blessed and holy is the one who has a part in the first resurrection; over these the second death has no power, but they will be priests of God and Christ and will reign with him for a thousand years.

I believe the first resurrection is reserved for those who matured first, those who attained a high calling in Christ, and evidently, these are the ones God will use to usher in his Kingdom on earth.

John 5: 28–29 tells us a little more about the second resurrection: "Do not marvel at this, for an hour is coming when all who are in the tombs will hear his voice and come out, those who have done good to the resurrection of life,"— to be made alive, vivified—"and those who have done evil to the resurrection of judgment." (ESV) This can't pertain to the first resurrection, because that one was limited.

Revelation 20:12–15 gives us a little more insight into the second resurrection: "And I saw the dead, the great and small, standing before the throne, and the books were opened: and another book was opened, which is the book of life; and the dead were judged from the things which were written in the books, according to their deeds . . . And death and Hades were thrown into the lake of fire. This is the second death. And if anyone's name was not found written in the book of life, he was thrown into the lake of fire." (ESV) In the second general resurrection, those found in the book of life are vivified, just like the first group, and allowed to live on in God's Kingdom. Others, not found in the book, are thrown into the lake of fire, and this is the second death.

Please understand that being brought to life is not a guarantee of life without death. Some have been raised in the past, but died later. In the Greek language, "resurrected" and "vivified" are two different words. Jesus promises something very special for the first group and those who belong to him in the second group—he makes them alive; he vivifies them to the point where death no longer holds power over them.

So far, I see two resurrections with two different squadrons of people being made alive. The first one includes those who will rule and reign with him for a thousand years, the firstfruits. I believe they will receive the honor of what other scriptures refer to as aionian life, which indicates age-lasting life or activity in his Kingdom. The second squadron includes those whose names were found in the book of life, those who are Christ's at his coming, and they are also vivified, just later.

But what about the rest who were raised in the second resurrection but not found in the book of life, those who do not belong to him at the time of his coming? The record states these are sentenced to the second death in the lake of fire. Many theologians close the book at this point and consider the matter settled because verse twenty-four states, "then the end, when he delivers the kingdom to God the Father."

However, other theologians see it differently, for there is evidence that the phrase, "then the end" could have been, "then, the remainder." In either case, I see both phrases referring to the end of the squadrons, the last group to be vivified, the last harvest, the remainder of humanity. After all, if Paul starts his argument in verse twenty-two emphatically stating that all men are included in Christ, the super set, how in God's name could he leave out what some consider being the largest group of men to have ever lived, non-Christians/non-believers?

Leaving out most of humanity from the groups is what I call Louisiana logic. One of my first trips with UPS outside of my home state was to Louisiana. A group of us went there to audit and approve the District's request to install a bonus system for their drivers in Natchitoches. And just how do you pronounce the name of that city? Going there, I thought it might be pronounced somewhat like it is spelled, "Nat chi to ches." Nope! I learned from the locals that it's pronounced, "Nacodish." Just how they arrived at that pronunciation was my first introduction to Louisiana logic, at least according the leader of our group at the time, our Regional I.E. Manager, Gerry Geisler.

Gerry was a very bright engineer who had been promoted from the New York area to be in charge of the Southwest Region, which included Texas, New Mexico, Oklahoma, Arkansas, and Louisiana. Not only was Gerry super intelligent, he was also very direct and absolutely hilarious at times, especially after a few drinks. Later during the week, after returning to the District's home office in New Orleans, all of the auditors and some of the local engineers went for a brisk walk with him to get some evening exercise before the eating and drinking festivities began later in the evening. Gerry was a fanatic about walking and was in excellent shape. I don't know exactly where we were at the time, but we walked through a Lake Pontchartrain neighborhood where there were what looked to be million dollar homes. As I walked, I remember making a comment to him about how beautiful the park-like area was but how nervous I'd be about building there with the water level of the lake being noticeably higher than the habitat of the homes. Gerry went off: "That's more of that Louisiana logic, son! One of these days a hurricane is going to blow that water over these levies and it's going to deep-six all of these houses! These people are crazy, but they sure know how to cook!" Everyone laughed.

We had a scrumptious Cajun dinner later that evening and Gerry continued to entertain us with his candor and humor. Later, he would tell us how crazy Texans were too, including the wildlife. He said he had noticed in his short time living in Texas a significant number of crazy varmints, namely armadillos, the only animal he knew that slept calmly on the roads with their feet straight up in the air. Weren't they worried about getting run over? For the rest of my career, when engineering mistakes were discovered, we, including my engineering friends from Louisiana, often referred it to as "Louisiana logic."

That humor came to end after the indescribable amount of suffering for those who experienced Katrina. Our hearts were broken after their incredible loss. However, the idea that most of humanity will be left out of God's plan for redemption only to suffer eternally after being overcome by another well-known lake is an infinitely more horrible thought. This line of reasoning pales in comparison to Louisiana logic. I know this may sound harsh, but in my view, this logic is more in line with what ISIS believes than with Paul's teaching. If you don't believe the way they do, these Islamic extremists will burn you alive without regard to the sanctity of life or the genuineness of your beliefs. The world looks on with horror, including many Christians who fail to see the repulsiveness of their own belief that their god will give up on most of humanity and sentence them to eternal flames and annihilation.

Even though I see this last group as having the sad distinction of an unyielding heart at the time of his second coming, and even though they will have to endure judgment in the lake of fire, whatever that is, I believe it will only be for a season until they become repentant. At that time they will be rescued in love and join the other two groups in peace and harmony with God and all others. Remember the beginning of Paul's treatise: "even so in Christ shall all be made alive." Remember the end of it too: "that God may be all in all."

Just who belongs in the third group is an interesting study, which we will not discuss in detail here. However, when you have the time, I urge you to find out who Jesus called His enemies. To be clear, I no longer believe this group includes all non-believers at the time of His coming, for I do not see the Gandhi's of this world as being His enemies, and I do see hope for them as being part of the second group. What I have found is that His enemies are the self-righteous who considered themselves to be the elite among us. They are those who took advantage of others because of their lack of love for them and a lack of love for their Heavenly Father. For those, a change of heart is required, and consequently, they will be the last to enter the Kingdom of Peace as the scriptures promise, "the first shall be last." As my friend Mike warns, if you plan to read your resume' to Him on judgment day, take your shoes off and put your trunks on; you might be taking a swim in a very warm lake.

In support of the idea of three squadrons who are eventually vivified, a fascinating study can be done surrounding the three major feast celebrations of Israel—the Feast of Passover, the Feast of Pentecost, and the Feast of Tabernacles. Below is what I learned about them from Dr. Jones.

Three times a year men were to "appear before the Lord God" and "celebrate a festival unto me." Each one of the festivals was associated with the harvest of a certain crop. The first celebration was the Feast of Passover. Barley was harvested at this time. As a crop, it matured first. And in Leviticus we find the barley being mixed with oil, anointed if you will, and cooked in "an offering by fire to the Lord." As a firstfruit, it was consecrated to the Lord as an earnest or pledge of the full harvest yet to be gathered.

And remember how Jesus fed the masses with loaves of barley? Isn't that our calling as firstfruits to be a living sacrifice in service to others? The barley squadron appears to represent those who mature first in Christ. They represent the high calling that Paul said he was striving towards.

The next celebration was the Feast of Pentecost. Wheat was harvested at this time, and in Leviticus 29 we find two loaves of flour mixed with leaven and offered to God. Our efforts to serve him were full of leaven— the imperfections of our own efforts, like this book as an example. But he knows that. And even though we may not qualify to rule and reign with him, as a merciful Father, he fully intends to harvest this crop and give this squadron vivification too.

The last celebration was the Feast of Tabernacles. In Numbers 29 we read the Feast of Tabernacles began with the sacrifice of thirteen bullocks on the first day, twelve on the next, then eleven . . . all the way down to seven. The total sacrificed was seventy. So what is God saying with all these numbers? Thirteen is a number that is symbolic of rebellion; seven is perfection, and seventy is restoration. So here's the story behind the numbers for the third and final group - what began in rebellion, ends in perfection, for the purpose of restoration.

In Nehemiah 8 we find the Israelites returning to Jerusalem after Babylonian captivity. At the time of the Feast of Tabernacles, we find them gathering with all Israelites and strangers in the land to read the law. At this point, they stood together, read it, and said, "Amen" in unity. The significance here is that everyone had found knowledge and agreement with God's ways. With hearts and minds changed, we will be fully prepared to live in peace and harmony together.

Grapes were harvested at the last feast celebration of Tabernacles. And what did they do with grapes after harvesting them? They stomped them under their feet. And notice the continuing language in our Corinthians passage, "then comes the end/remainder, when he delivers the kingdom to God the Father, when he puts an end to all authority and power. For he must reign until he puts all things under his feet." The grapes appear to be the enemies of Christ in this present world. And Paul comes back to the "under the feet" theme several times until he ends in verse twenty-eight with, "that God may be all in all." I believe this is the third and final squadron, the last harvest, the remainder to be vivified. He also added in verse twenty-six after all groups had been vivified, that death is finally destroyed.

I'm so amazed at the harmony of language and ideas used in the scriptures. No man could ever put it together that well. And it continues. The first part of God's communion is to serve the bread, which represents his body, us, the barley and wheat harvests. We are to offer ourselves as a living sacrifice with him as the bread of life in us. But his communion is not complete until the grapes, his enemies, have been harvested as well.

In summary, we have found three squadrons of men, three feast celebrations, three harvests, three crops, three vivifications at three different times, and consequently, three views of heaven; I call this pattern of threes the divine *passacaglia*. (ital)

To highlight all of these layers of threes, I believe Jesus made a very prophetic statement in Luke 13:32. Below are three different translations of it:

New International Version (NIV) He replied, "Go tell that fox, 'I will keep on driving out demons and healing people today and tomorrow, and on the third day I will reach my goal.'"

New Living Translation (NLT) "Jesus replied, 'Go tell that fox that I will keep on casting out demons and healing people today and tomorrow; and the third day I will accomplish my purpose.'"

English Standard Version (ESV) And he said to them, "Go and tell that fox, 'Behold, I cast out demons and perform cures today and tomorrow, and the third day I finish my course.'" The casting out demons is the removal of evil and anything which stands in opposition to God's will in us. And in *A Generous Orthodoxy*, Brian McLaren, founding pastor of Cedar Ridge Community Church in Baltimore and author of *Finding Faith*, wrote: "In the Bible, 'save' means to 'rescue' or 'heal.'" With this understanding, we find Jesus sending a prophetic message to Herod, a prince and power of this world standing in opposition to his work. He said to tell that rascal (devil) that I'm going to cast evil out of men and save them today; I'm going to do it again tomorrow, but on the third time around, I'll reach perfection by saving them all. In doing so, his Kingdom will come and his will, will be accomplished, for He came not to condemn the world but to save it. And in the study of Bible numerics, scholars tell us the number "3" signifies "divine completeness and perfection."

But what about those unutterable things Paul heard when he was caught up to the third heaven? What did he hear? One plausible explanation is that Paul was told not to speak what he had heard because it would have disrupted the training and drawn the immature to Christ for all the wrong reasons. Think back to a time when Jesus told someone not to tell others about one of his miraculous accomplishments. How about the time when he healed a man but told him not to tell anyone? Why do you suppose he would make such a demand? I believe Jesus knew that if others found out about it, many would come to him for all the wrong reasons—for the miracles only. Plus, it was not time for him to heal everyone; there was still more training to do.

Personally, I believe what Paul heard were God's former enemies giving him praise and honor, something most Christians today could never imagine this group doing. For those who only see two groups being vivified, adding the third would be unthinkable, unspeakable, and therefore, unutterable—the richness of his kindness exceeding their expectations far beyond what they would ever dare dream.

We may never know what these unutterable things were until we see Paul on the other side. However, what we do know is that Jesus is more interested in changing hearts and minds than in satisfying the flesh with a display of his power. He was, and remains, more interested in the long term—making us like him from the inside out.

That's how I see it, and that's what I'm going with until God provides something better. All of us could be totally wrong about our interpretation of scripture here, but I love the fact that we have been given the opportunity to think for ourselves and talk to the Lord about it. I appreciate our great teacher allowing us to work on the problem and discover some amazing insights in scriptures that are far too coincidental to ignore. In time, these revelations open up like the bloom of a flower, and their beauty and fragrance are so stunning.

If anyone has anything to add, or if you see some errors in what I just presented, please let me know; I'm still learning and open for more.

11

May You Run

~

While writing this book some of those closest to me, who knew the direction I wanted to take it, asked me why I had allowed someone else to write most of chapter nine in a book that was supposed to be my memoir. That was a fair question and my response was, "This book is more than a memoir." It's a spiritual odyssey and Mike's story expressed my struggles better than I could have done—just like George Jones could sing the blues better than anyone, at least in my opinion. Even though at times I may have felt the same degree of passion that George sang about, I know we'd all rather listen to George sing than me. The words "he stopped loving her today" are forever etched in my memory, which brings me to the second reason for using Mike's pen—to drive home a point that our stories are intertwined for our mutual benefit, if we allow them to be. They must be told to hold a spot in more than one memory bank, or else those we care about will lose the advantage. Mike's journey has definitely influenced me and his pilgrimage has become a significant part of my spiritual journey.

I can't overemphasize the importance of telling your story. I've established a website to host your story, your journey written in your own words, at PassItForward.Life. What you've learned can have a profound impact on others, even those you may never meet on this side of eternity. Two such men recorded their stories and I hope one day I'll be able to thank them in person for their contribution to my development. They are Job and Dan Allender, PhD.

"I have uttered what I did not understand; things too wonderful for me, which I did not know . . . I have heard of You by the hearing of the ear, but now my eye sees You. Therefore . . . I repent." Job 42:3–6

A lot can be learned from the trials of Job. He didn't understand why all the evil had happened to him. But eventually he "saw" and repented for having thought so poorly of God. From what Job confessed, his prior understanding of God was, well, wrong. At least in some aspects. This is surprising considering the record's portrayal of a man who clearly held a deep and abiding reverence for God. Or is it?

When we look closely at the lives of other "religious" men, like the Pharisee of Pharisees, Saul, or even those closest to Jesus, like James and John, we find times when they were completely out of step with God's plan and purposes. If that is true, then, why should it be surprising to find times when we, as individuals, or even as a church collectively, need to change our minds and re-group? This is one of the great lessons we can take from Job.

As an example, and as given by my friend Randy Klassen, in 1845 the Baptist General Convention recognized the need for change and issued a statement no longer approving the institution of slavery. However, a group of them rejected the statement, broke away, and formed the largest Protestant denomination in our country, the Southern Baptist Convention. It took almost 150 years before *that* group made an official apology, and racism still lingers among us to this day. To be fair, the Catholic Church has sheepishly made some changes down though their history as well.

And before we continue with the story of Job, here's another story where God's people ended up on the wrong end of the candle because of their misunderstanding of the One who chose them to be a light in the world—the Jews at Thessalonica. This Greek city was located in Macedonia, part of Alexander the Great's original kingdom. It was named after Alexander's half-sister, just like Philippi was named after Alexander's father. When the Apostle Paul came to the area, the whole region was saturated with the memories of a man who was not only a military conquer, but may also have been the first universalist according to scholar William Barclay. Alexander valued freedom and equality, and he dreamed of an empire where there was neither Greek, nor Jew, nor barbarian or Scythian, nor bond or free. The supreme importance of the city lay in its location as a gateway between the east and west. It was a free city having never seen Roman troops quartered within its boundary. The trading industry made it a thriving metropolis and its population rose to 200,000. For a time, it was competing with Constantinople as the recognized capital of the world. Paul knew the coming of

Christianity to this great city was crucial to spreading the good news of the gospel—the grace, peace, freedom and liberty we have in Christ.

From its history and culture, the setting was ripe for harvest, but guess who stood in the way of this great message? Those who should have known better—God's chosen people. The Jews were so enraged with Paul's success in teaching God's grace for all men through the sacrifice of his Son that he had to be smuggled out of the city after about three weeks. The same thing happened in Berea, where Paul had to leave Timothy and Silas in charge and escape to Athens.

Paul feared so much about what might happen to the flock in Thessalonica that when Timothy joined him in Athens, he immediately sent him back to get more information about their condition. And Timothy brought back great news; they were standing fast in the faith. In a second letter to those babes in Christ, Paul told the flock that God would repay those who had afflicted them. The KJV translates it this way: "In flaming fire taking vengeance on them that know not God"—and who was troubling these guys because they were on the wrong side of God's plan?—". . .who shall be punished with everlasting destruction from the presence of the Lord."

I am really bothered by the poor translation of this passage and the amount of misinformation promoted by those locked in tradition. They attempt to apply this verse to all non-believers when it was specifically aimed at God's chosen—Jews who were hanging on to the old covenant and standing in the way of the age of grace. You already know what I think about the mistranslation of the word "everlasting." But going even further off the mark, several modern translations have erroneously added the word "away" in front of " from the presence of the Lord" leaving the casual reader with the idea that those receiving this judgment are removed eternally away from the presence of the Lord. However, correction that comes "from the presence of the Lord" does the exact opposite as in the case of Saul and as will be the case for the Jews.

In the eleventh chapter of Romans, Paul tells us an amazing story of how God uses Israel's falling away to bring in the rest of the nations, and then promises a day "when all Israel shall be saved" too. Paul sees this plan as one where God has committed "all (both Jews and Gentiles) to disobedience that he may have mercy on all." In front of that statement, Paul reminds us that the gift (of faith) and the calling (as in the case of the Jews to be instruments in his hand) "are irrevocable." If I'm worked-up over the richness of his kindness, it's nothing compared to the way Paul ends his discourse to the believers in Rome:

"Oh, the depth of the riches of the wisdom and knowledge of God! How unsearchable are his judgments and his ways past finding out! For who has known the mind of the Lord? Or who has become his counselor? Or who has first given to him and it shall be repaid to him? For of him and through him and to him are all things, to whom be glory forever. Amen."

Now, let's get back to Job after having placed Protestants, Catholics and Jews all in the same basket—at least at some point in their history when they were wrong. A genuinely tough question to answer is whether or not Job would have learned as much about himself, others and God if he had not gone through as much hell as he did. It is a sobering and uncomfortable thought that many of the important lessons in this life cannot be learned apart from genuine, heartfelt loss and trials. Further, what is seldom pointed out is the possibility that what Job went through may actually have been more for the benefit of posterity than for him—for the millions of readers who would follow him and contemplate more deeply the purposes of his ordeals vis-à-vis understanding God. Only after a tremendous amount of struggle did God opened Job's eyes to hidden purposes in all things, including his experiences with evil. Listen to his words that followed: "therefore . . . I repent . . ."—for having thought so poorly of God. I was wrong not to trust him. In fact, Job had earlier declared an amazing level of trust: "Though he slay me, yet will I trust in him." We suspect that by the end of his ordeal, Job found a new appreciation for even his own words! And we further suspect that he found more depth in his commitment than ever before.

Remember, the word used for *repentance* has the fundamental meaning of changing the mind. Job changed his mind about God's plan for him and his family. At that point, he began to trust God in every circumstance. Not only was Job's mind changed, but God also left a record to help billions of *others* struggling to make sense of the difficulties and disappointments in this life and how they *may* relate to God's activities. God used Job and his family to bless us with the comfort of knowing that he is in control, no matter how poor our circumstances on earth may become. Not every calamity in life is a result of some sin committed by that person. Yes, sometimes we deliberately screw up and we have to suffer the consequences of our own choices and poor decisions, but to me, that's elementary stuff compared to what God is teaching us through Job.

May You Run

In what I call the epilog to the book of Job, Jesus healed a man born blind. John chapter nine records the healing. The question Jesus received from his disciples, perhaps thousands of years after the events of Job, shows how little things change in the human condition. Upon seeing the man and his condition, they asked him, "Rabbi, who sinned, this man or his parents, that he was born blind?" (John 9:2). I hate to think that Job's sufferings were in vain, but based on their question, it really makes me wonder. Fortunately, Jesus rebuked the presumption in the question and told them that maybe, just maybe, God had other purposes for the man's condition that had nothing to do with sin—his or his parents: "'Neither this man nor his parents sinned,' said Jesus, 'but this happened so that the work of God might be displayed in his life.'" (John 9:3). Sadly, we think Jesus's response may well have stunned his disciples. We need to understand that every life, every circumstance, and every story plays an important role in the development of mankind. Apparently, God is quite the story-teller, and his stories are interwoven with all manner of difficulties. That being the case, do you trust him? Is he good? Are such difficulties meant for your good, or for your evil? Are your sufferings meant *only* to teach you something? Or could it be, just like Job, there are *those around you* who are being blessed because of your circumstances?

Dr. Dan Allender, a noted Christian counselor, wrote a book called *The Healing Path*. After years of counseling, he identified four routes Christians commonly take when dealing with difficulties in their life. Instead of seeking to grow in faith, hope and love, all four of them seek to put the blame for life's pain on chance, the enemy, and other men, instead of crediting and assuming that God has a real purpose for putting us in such trials. Allender concluded, "As men and women after God's own heart, we are called to walk the path that Jesus walked. Isaiah 53:3 states he was a man of sorrows acquainted with grief and familiar with suffering. The road to Golgotha was full of temptations to side-step death, yet Jesus learned obedience through suffering. His choice to embrace the battles resulted in victory over death, and we are called to that same journey."

Allender challenges Christians to recall because every one of us has a *unique* story of God's redemptive intervention in our lives. Whether we realize it or not, God is telling a story, his story in us. He is intimately involved in every moment of your day. Allender describes how God orchestrates and tells our story as the author and narrator. "Faith increases to the degree that we are caught up, enthralled by, and participating in his story in ours." He reminds us that approximately 70 percent of the Bible is written in narrative form. "God is a story-teller who weaves his presence into every story in the Bible. And how does he God tell a story? With drama. He tells stories that excite, confuse, entice, disrupt, and change the human heart. Drama involves a beginning, with a setting, characters, and a search or problem to be solved, then, a middle with a plot that has moments of tragedy that brings a rise in tension and risk that demands faith, then an ending that instills confidence and invigorates hope." If we realize his story in ours, we can confidently face any challenge in life, no matter the difficulty, because we know what awaits us beyond this moment.

While speaking and consulting with Mike about the contents of this final chapter, he asked if he could add a few paragraphs and I gladly said yes. I did not know the contents would include a few compliments, and I'm glad the Father's training is beginning to show some results, even in me. The following is from Mike Meeker:

MIKE MEEKER ON DYING IN VAIN

The Vangelis theme song from Costa-Gavras' movie *Missing* is playing just now on my iPod. I think of the loss of life of a young man the film depicted. Was his death in vain? Our faith says no. Did Abraham Lincoln die in vain? Our faith wants us to say no. Yet, every fiber in the secular world would have us conclude that it's "Vanity—all is vanity." What about those near and dear to you—those you have lost, was it all in vain? Were their lives a waste of time? We believe not. We declare not.

At the end of the previous chapter, I examined four possible reasons God has so ordered existence upon this planet the way it is. I commend them to your conscience for reflection and contemplation before the trials of life come calling. As I read through that section again, I realized I had left out one other piece of the story. I forgot to tell the reader how my trials have affected me. I won't spend much ink on the matter but one fundamental truth I can tell you is that I now know what the meaning of the phrase, "peace that passes all understanding" actually means. I know how it arrived. I know how it sustains me now. I know now nothing can take me out of his hands. I know his affections for me are limitless. I know his position to all mankind is encapsulated in the Gospel—Grace and Peace to you from the God and Father of Our Lord Jesus Christ! I now know how out of place my anger against God was and much like the blindness

Job's friends were crippled by, my anger against him for all my sufferings were based on a false understanding of who he is.

Unfortunately, my understanding was given me by the church I grew up in. Oh, don't get me wrong, those who taught me meant well, I'm sure. And I'm sure they thought the view of God they taught me was, no doubt, true. But like Bildad, Eliphaz, and Zophar before them, I now think these people who mentored me as a child never had a clue who God really was or is. I suspect that is the case for many believers—they are affected by the view of God they received as children well into adulthood. But praise God, I have now been freed to rest in his grace and to know that my destiny is bright, my future secure because of who he really is—the God who loves just because that is his essence. I don't have to earn his love, his affections or his good will towards me. he has given these to me for all time.

Nothing can change his view of me. And the peace that realization has brought me is that which I wish every heart knew. Now, like Paul, I am determined that I will not return to where I once stood—to that angry view of God, to that bondage of trying to prove my righteousness before God by my works and I am therefore, determined not to "frustrate the grace of God: for if righteousness come by the Law, then Christ died" for no purpose. I now want to serve him—not out of fear—but out of affection for him and have determined to live the life "which I now live in the flesh" by the "faith of the Son of God, who loved me, and gave himself for me." My essence now rests in peace—the anger and fear are gone now. But I'll let you in on a little secret. That idea that his love, his affections and his good will towards me will never change—is also true for every person that has ever been or will ever be.

My friend Jim, told me a story a few years back which had a profound and lasting beneficial effect on me. In one year, he endured the deaths of a number of his family members—two that immediately come to my mind. He would never admit to it, but he has a calmness about him that is infectious. I was concerned for his state because he had been through so much grief during that time. Instead of exhibiting any wrath or rancor, a weakness I might well have succumbed to, he told me that even though the end of our days will probably be as horrific as those who had just died within that year—that he was convinced that God would make good on the training for them and himself. I never told Jim just how profound that statement was to me—I really should work harder on my communication skills.

By extension, I now realize that whatever I go through—no matter how horrific it may be—my confidence, like his, is rooted in the expectation that the

King of Heaven will make good on his promises. He will not let my losses be in vain. And Jim and I will find that the real "author of this work," that is, our lives and destiny, turned out to be him all along, telling a story through our lives. And extending this confidence, we now believe that God is doing the same thing for everyone else and that they will likewise come to this same realization one day, Praise God! And Paul assures us "He that spared not his own Son, but delivered him up for us all, how shall he not with him also give freely us all things?" I swapped the word order of the KJV here because the verb Paul used is the verb form of the noun—wait for it—grace! His unmerited favor and peace given freely to us as noted above is the Gospel. In fact, we even think that by the time he is finished with us all—far from having to throw billions into Hell or to snuff out the existence of the "sinners" by annihilation, every person who had anger against him will come to find the words of the prophecy were just as true for them as it was for the House of Israel:

> But this cometh to pass, that the word might be fulfilled that is written in their law, They hated me without a cause. (John 15:25 KJV)

Of course, this implies a certain amount of fence-mending, restitution, judgment, healing and humility on the parts of all. Some of it we are looking forward to very much. As Jim told me once, "If I ever get the chance to meet Job and his children, I'm going to tell them how their losses helped me and countless others during our brief journey here on Earth." Wow! He's right, you know? These things we believe—these things we teach.

It's a very difficult journey to the Promised Land where we finally receive real freedom, the power that goes with it, and a new heart and mind motivated by love. And guess who will be waiting at the finish line praising and applauding our arrival? "Therefore judge nothing before the time, until the Lord come, Who both will bring to light the hidden things of darkness, and will make manifest the counsels of the hearts: and then shall every *one* have praise of God" (1 Corinthians 4:5, Rotherham's Emphasized Bible). "then applause will be coming to each one from God" (Concordant Literal New Testament). Imagine that; he will be clapping for you and me.

This is our God; this is our destiny. No one could pull off something so difficult and complex except him—bringing into maturity all of his sons and daughters. It is truly miraculous. I love this quote from Joseph Smith Dodge (1834–1921): "The Savior cannot desist from his reconciling work until every soul that God has made shall be, through all its depths, in harmony with him. The task is vast and difficult beyond conception, and its accomplishment would be plainly impossible if it were committed to any weaker hands than those of the Son of God." The brightness around him is not only a reflection of his goodness, but it is also a manifestation of his intellectual brilliance.

His holy Word gives us a beautiful picture when his reality—his finished work—becomes our reality. Isaiah 25:6–9: "And in this mountain [the gospel] shall the Lord make unto all people a feast of fat things; . . . and he will destroy in this mountain the covering cast over the face of all people, and the veil that is spread over all nations. He will swallow up death in victory; and the Lord God will wipe away tears from off all faces; and the rebuke of his people shall he take away from off all the earth: for the Lord hath spoken it. And it shall be said in that day, Lo, this is our God; we have waited for him, and he will save us: this is the Lord; we have waited for him, we will be glad, and rejoice in his salvation." (KJV)

A friend recently gave me a blue decorative pillow with the inscription "Love never fails." And if I don't live to see his second coming, I've made a request that my head is laid to rest on that pillow when this portion of my journey on earth is over. It's a powerful statement and I'll continue to rest comfortably in his promises long after I'm gone. I pray that same comfort for any and all I encounter in this life.

In summary, this book is my best attempt at describing our God. But what I've seen in the brightness around him is not what is most important; it's what you see. If you are not sure who he is, or what he is like, then, I wish you Godspeed on your path of discovery. I encourage you to go to him now in prayer; go to him quickly; may you run, for this is the One you've been waiting for. And for the rest of us who have already caught a glimpse of his goodness, I pray our lives will be a continuous reflection of that goodness in all we say and do.

Epilogue

In This Moment

~

God's Word tells us that He resides in Temples not made with hands—you and I. That means we don't really "go to church," because church is wherever we find ourselves. The message we deliver from our pulpits, and the songs of praise we sing from our hearts, are found in everyday conversations with others. And our tithes and offerings are measured by the kindness, compassion and help we give to those around us. May your Temple offer peace, hope and love to those in the community of your life as you reflect, *The Brightness Around Him*.

Speaking of songs from our hearts, I don't know if Chris Tomlin agrees with me or not, but the lyrics to his song, *God's Great Dance Floor*, certainly does. The words resonate with all I wish to leave you with: *"Take me; this is all I can bring... You'll never stop loving us, no matter how far we run; you'll never give up on us. All of heaven shouts, let the future begin! I feel alive; I come alive; I am alive on God's great dance floor!"* You'll find the rest of the words and the song at http://www.godtube.com/watch/?v=W7PGDLNX.

Also, whenever I need inspiration, I love listening to one of the greatest songs of our day found in Danny Gokey's *Hope In Front of Me*. You can hear him sing it at http://www.youtube.com/watch?v=9KIhYZQ_ovw. In my opinion, few songs are as powerful as this one.

Thank you Heavenly Father from the bottom of my heart for this wonderful journey. I know I've been far from perfect and will always be grateful that You never gave up on me. Please take this book and make it all it can be for this is all I can bring.

In This Moment

To all the authors quoted and mentioned in this book, thank you for your sacrifices and time spent encouraging and inspiring us. Below are some great books written by a few of them:

- *The Divine Reversal* by Caleb Miller
- *What Does The Bible Really Say About Hell?* By Randy Klassen
- *The Inescapable Love of God* by Thomas Talbott
- *Spiritual Terrorism: Spiritual Abuse from the Womb to the Tomb* by Boyd Purcell, PhD
- *Christianity Without Insanity* by Boyd Purcell, PhD
- *The Evangelical Universalist* by Gregory MacDonald (Robin Parry)
- *The One Purpose of God* by Jan Bonda
- *Christ Triumphant* by Thomas Allin
- *Restitution of All Things* by Andrew Jukes
- *Love Wins* by Rob Bell
- *Hope Beyond Hell* by Gerry Beauchemin
- *Hope for ALL Generations and Nations* by Gary Amirault
- *All In All* by A.E. Knoch
- *The Problem of Evil and the Judgments of God* by A.E. Knoch
- *Today, Tomorrow, & The Great Beyond* by John S. Fox
- *The Insanity In Christianity* by Dr. JV Foster
- *Every Knee Shall Bow* by Thomas Allin and Mark T. Chamberlain
- *Sacred Secrets of the Sovereignty of God* by James Walter Bruggeman
- *At the End of the Ages—The Abolition of Hell* by Bob Evely
- *Creation's Jubilee* by Dr. Stephen Jones
- *The Laws of the Second Coming* by Dr. Stephen Jones
- *Universal Salvation? The Current Debate* edited by Robin Parry & Christopher H. Partridge
- *The First Idiot in Heaven* by Martin Zender
- *Is God Fair? What About Gandhi?* By Michael Riley and James William[/BL 1-24]

Please visit IsGodFair.com, and PassItForward.life

In This Moment

There are also some great websites to visit with plenty of material to consider. For example, the first one has some great articles concerning the lake of fire and those who contradict.

- Bible-truths.com
- Tentmaker.org
- Studyshelf.com
- Darroll.tripod.com
- Hopebeyondhell.net
- IsGodfair.com
- AlexanderThomson.blogspot.com

And to the readers of this book—thank you for your time and patience. I hope you will write and tell me your story—I love reading God's dramas. Remember, your story is not just for you; it's also to help the rest of us with our training. To that end, I'm planning to start a new web site to include personal stories about what God has taught you. With your permission, I will post them for your family and friends to enjoy. Just send me an email, and I'll send you more details. You don't need to write a book, just leave behind in writing what you want others to know. You can reach me at: jameswilliam@isgodfair.com. I'm looking forward to hearing from you.

Lastly, a special thanks goes out to new age and "chill-out" artists Patrick O'Hearn, Ryan Farish, Ryan Stewart, David Lanz and Paul Speer, David Helpling, Blank & Jones, and others like them. I really enjoy their smooth and easy style of music, and every chapter title in this book is named after some of their work. As a matter of fact, I feel so relieved to have finally finished this book, I think I'll go relax and count some clouds. Care to join me? http://www.youtube.com/watch?v=K3Ibun_gc88

Appendix

Notes from Let's Talk Bible

~

MULTIPLE TRANSLATIONS OF OLAM

The definition of *olam* from Hebrew dictionary in *Strong's Concordance*: It is used 448 times in the Old Testament. It is derived from *alam* which according to Strong means "to veil from sight, to conceal, literally or figuratively." Bullinger in his appendix calls *olam* a hidden time or hidden age—indefinite or obscure time. We agree with Bullinger. Ecc 3:11 makes this point perfectly clear. *Olam* is a time period that is hidden from our understanding. Strong agrees, calling it concealed time—generally time past or future—but then adds: practically speaking "eternity." Really? Hmmm.

Some obvious errors when translating it as eternity: Exodus 21:6 (KJV): "a slave forever"? The NIV and Revised Standard say "for life." Then Exodus 40:15 (KJV) declares the Priesthood of Aaron to be "everlasting"? The Revised Standard says "perpetual," and the NIV "for all generations to come." Again the idea of forever. However, the weaker Aaronic Priesthood was replaced by a stronger order after Melchizedek. Hebrews 7:11-12. Kings 9: 1–3—Solomon's Temple lasted about 400 years

These are just a few more examples of the KJV and others assigning eternity to *olam*, when it was obviously a finite period. We won't go into all of the examples, but we will summarize with a quote from Thomas Thayer:

> In the Old Testament we see the word everlasting applied to the priesthood of Aaron; to the mountains and hills; and to the doors of the Jewish temple. We see the word forever applied to the duration of a man's earthly existence; to the time a child was to abide in

the temple; to the continuance of Gehazi's leprosy; to the duration of the life of David; to the duration of a king's life; to the time the Jews were to possess the land of Canaan; to the time they were to dwell in Jerusalem; to the time a servant was to abide with his master; to the duration of the Jewish temple; to the time David was to be king over Israel; to the throne of Solomon; to the stones that were set up at Jordan; and to the time Jonah was in the fish's belly. We find the phrase forever and ever applied to the sun, moon, and stars; to a writing contained in a book; to the smoke that went up from the burning land of Idumea; and to the time the Jews were to dwell in Judea. We find the word never applied to the time the fire was to burn on the Jewish altar; to the time the sword was to remain in the house of David; to the time the Jews should not experience shame; to the time the house of David was to reign over Israel; to the time the Jews were not to open their mouths because of their shame; and to the time judgment was not executed.

But the priesthood of Aaron and his sons has ceased; the Jews had for a long time been driven from the land of Canaan, and God has brought upon them a reproach and a shame; the man to the duration of whose life the word forever was applied is dead; David is dead, and has ceased to reign over Israel; the throne of Solomon no longer exists; the Jewish temple is demolished, the Temple was destroyed, the servants of the Jews have been freed from their masters; Gehazi is dead, and no one believes he carried his leprosy with him into the future world; the stones that were set up at Jordan have been removed, and the smoke that went up from the burning land of Idumea has ceased to ascend; no one believes that the mountains and hills, as such, are indestructible; the fire that burnt on the Jewish altar has long since ceased to burn; and some judgments have been executed.

Here's more trouble for *olam* as eternity: the word "eternity" is doubled in eleven places. If *olam* is forever, why is it doubled up eleven times? So should we take 1 Chronicles 16:36 as poetic language, or is it a wrong translation? We say it should have been rendered "from the age and unto the age."

Another question for King James: why is *olam* also used eleven times in the plural? For example 1 Kings 8:13 "forever" is "forevers" in the original. (The translators treated the singular and plural forms of this word as if they were the same). More poetry, or should it have been "unto the ages"?

The KJV translators were inconsistent elsewhere too. Isaiah 45:17 translates a double-*olam* as "everlasting" and "world without end." *Olam va ad*—eternity and beyond? How about "to the age and beyond"? Other places they used "ancient times" and "old times" because everlasting would not fit (see Joshua 24:2).

MULTIPLE TRANSLATIONS OF AION

Now let's go to the New Testament where the questions and inconsistencies for the uses of *aion* are just as obvious. Greek equivalent of *olam* is *aion*: Septuagint (translation from Hebrew to Greek) shows they are equivalent. The New Testament often quotes the Old Testament (see Hebrews 1:8 with Psalm 45:6, and Hebrews 5:6 with Psalm 110:4).

Strong's definition of *aion*: "An age, by extension—perpetuity, by implication—the world."

Really? That's like saying the word "dry" means not wet, but by extension "wet," or "black" means by extension "white."

In the parable of the unrighteous manager, those of the "mammon of unrighteousness" don't have the ability to accept you into "eternal" habitations. Only God can do that. (CT John 14:2) This is yet another piece of the evidence that *aiwnios* should never have been translated as eternal.

Talk about inconsistency: in the first three chapters of Ephesians we find *aion* translated six times in the KJV as follows: world, course, ages, beginning of the world, eternal, and world without end. How does one word carry so many meanings? "Age or ages would have worked perfectly in all instances.

Of the 197 times used, *aion* is found in its noun form about 128 times and adjective forms about 71 times. About one-third of the time they are used in the singular, and about two-thirds in the plural, or in the context of the plural. For example in Matthew 12:32 the KJV used "world" because in this verse "forever" or "the forever to come" would not work. How about "neither in this age nor the age to come"? The NIV correctly uses age.

The argument whether *aion* can be translated as world or not can be settled by the words of Jesus in Mathew 13:38–40. Here he interprets his own parable, saying "the field is the *kosmos* (world) . . . and the harvest is the end of the *aion* (age) . . . so shall it be at the end of the *aion* (age)." The NIV & Revised Standard recognized the mistake and translated *aion* correctly as age.

The plural treated as the singular. 1 Cor 2:7 and 2 Tim 1:9 (it's *aions*—so why did the KJV use "world"?) NIV used "time" on this one.

Aions (eternities, according to the translators) also have beginnings in the verses above—and they have endings in Matthew 13 above! Need more proof? One *aion* follows another in Hebrews 1:2.

Then there's new math—as in more than one eternity in Hebrews 11:3. The KJV translates it as "worlds" ... more than one world? The NIV translates it as "universe." But the word is simply *aions*, or ages. So if the NIV and the Revised Standard knew from Mafthew 12:32 and 13: 38-40 that *aion* had to be age, why wouldn't they have translated the plural of age as "ages" instead of "universe"? Or why not "universes"?

The plural treated as singular. In 1 Corinthians 10:11 comes this strange phrase: "ends of the world." NIV got it right—"ages"! But why did they translate the exact same word in its plural form as "time" or "universe" in other places? This is very inconsistent.

OBJECTIONS IN TRANSLATING OLAM AND AION AS AGE

Used in relation to God, *aion* can mean eternity because it is used in relation to God. We know He is eternal, but does calling him the God of this age or the God of past ages or the ages to come restrict him from being an eternal God? Is the God of Abraham, Isaac and Jacob not the God of everyone? These types of expressions merely add emphasis to the fact that he is sovereign now in the present age just as he was in the past and will be in future.

First Timothy 1:17 "be honour and glory forever and ever." The closing phrase being *aionos ton aionon*. "Ton" means "of the" not "and." Holy of Holies, Song of Songs, King of Kings. Why not "ages of the ages"?

What about eternal life? Isn't that life in heaven? Some scholars argue *aionion* or the phrase *aionion life* does not usually denote endless existence, but the life of the gospel, spiritual life, the Christian life, regardless of duration. In more than fifty of the approximate seventy times the adjective occurs in the New Testament, it describes life. What is *aionion life*? Let the Scriptures answer. John 3:36, "He that believeth on the Son hath *aionion life*." John 5:24, "He that believeth on Him that sent me hath everlasting life, and shall not come into condemnation but is passed from death unto life." John 6:47, "He that believeth on me hath everlasting life." Repeated in verse 54.

Notes from Let's Talk Bible

John 17:3, "This is life eternal to know thee, the only true God, and Jesus Christ whom thou hast sent." *Aionion life* is the life of the gospel. It consists in knowing, loving and serving God. This life is of an indefinite length, so that the usage of the adjective in the New Testament is altogether in favor of giving the word the sense of limited duration. Hence Jesus does not say "he that believeth, in this life, shall enjoy endless happiness in the next, but hath *aionion life* and is passed from death unto life."

Another possible meaning for *aionion life*: Participation in the first resurrection: *The Laws of the Second Coming* by Dr. Stephen Jones (pgs 15–18)

ADDITIONAL DATA POINTS TO PONDER

The Feast of Trumpets prophesies of two resurrections

Revelation 20:4–6 The first trumpet blast at the first resurrection

John 5:82–29 and Revelation 20:11–15 The second trumpets

Philippians 3:10–16 Paul hopes for the first resurrection. We believe the promise of *aionion life* is for those who attain to the first resurrection.

www.ingramcontent.com/pod-product-compliance
Lightning Source LLC
Chambersburg PA
CBHW071440160426
43195CB00013B/1975